MANAGING
PRESENTATIONS
Communicating with Impact

Savita Bhan Wakhlu

Response Books
A division of Sage Publications
New Delhi/Thousand Oaks/London

First published in 2000 by

Response Books
A division of Sage Publications India Pvt Ltd
M–32, Greater Kailash Market–I
. New Delhi 110 048

Sage Publications Inc   Sage Publications Ltd
2455 Teller Road   6 Bonhill Street
Thousand Oaks, California 91320   London EC2A 4PU

Published by Tejeshwar Singh for Response Books, lasertypeset by Innovative Processors, New Delhi, and printed at Chaman Enterprises, Delhi.

Second Printing 2002

Library of Congress Cataloging-in-Publication Data

Wakhlu, Savita Bhan, 1959–
     Managing presentations: communicating with impact/
Savita Bhan Wakhlu.
        p. cm.
     Includes bibliographical references and index.
     1. Business presentations. I. Title

HF5718.22.W347 2000   658.4'5—dc21   00–062688

ISBN: 0–7619–9460–2   (US–PB)   81–7036–931–2   (India–PB)

Production Team: Sangeeta Goswami, R.A.M. Brown and Santosh Rawat

This book is dedicated to all those who are keen to become effective speakers and are continuously working on themselves.

CONTENTS

FOREWORD

With the advent of internet, e-commerce and various new modes of doing business, it has become increasingly important to communicate quickly and precisely. It is a fact that good ideas and penetrating analyses often get buried, because the one communicating these has not acquired the proper skills to get those ideas and thoughts across to an impatient world. It is those persons who will hold the attention of the reader/viewer, who can make their case as accurately as possible, and in the shortest possible time. The world now cannot tolerate long-winded and confusing presentations.

Time and clarity are of the essence, and are the hallmarks of a good communicator. Under such circumstances, it is necessary to sharpen one's skills to quickly hold the attention of the receiver, and ensure that this interest is maintained, till the message conveyed is completed. A logical flow of thoughts is very, very important. Therefore, the present book *Managing Presentations: Communicating with Impact* by Savita Bhan Wakhlu is apt, and to be welcomed.

I am confident that those who take advantage of this book, will acquire the skills that Savita has shown over the years. She has had experience in communicating with a wide variety of audiences, and has achieved a large degree of success in conducting courses connected with communication. I am sure that her experiences which have been put down in this book, will help those who read it, to communicate better, and with greater impact.

Jamshed J. Irani
Managing Director
Tata Steel
Jamshedpur

PREFACE

I still remember that afternoon, years ago, when my Standard VI English teacher told my mother that while I knew my course material well, I couldn't express it quite as clearly. My dear mother didn't know what to make of the feedback!

'If our daughter has prepared well, why can't she express herself?' I remember her asking my father. It was only years later that I fully understood the meaning of my teacher's comment.

My first experience of speaking before an audience occurred during my years of scholarship at the engineering college. A ten-minute talk on a technical topic, to be delivered in front of sixty odd individuals, was enough for me to experience the nervous symptoms associated with speaking in public. My intestines felt queasy, while my tongue was almost out of control, blurting out what was to be said at a frenetic pace! Despite this, the presentation was well received and I made the grade!

When I look back and analyze my first few experiences of speaking in public, I think I was able to make an impact on account of a few factors. First, was my command over the English language. Secondly, I never made any presentation without intense prior preparation. And finally, I always exhibited a positive and pleasing personality. I had the added advantage of knowing my audience well: after all, they were my classmates!

There were times, however, when I could have done better. In spite of being well-prepared, my delivery was often flawed. The weaknesses that led to such situations were largely psychological. An inability to control my nervousness and anxiety, being worried about the kind of questions that would be asked of me, and of course, anxiety about whether my talk would be appreciated by my audience or not.

A few months before I left college, I was to make a speech. This time the audience included a whole host of threatening faces. There were experienced faculty, students from other disciplines, and a smattering of unknown men and women. All of them seemed to be peering at me. This time, however, I was more confident thanks to one of my good friends, who had suggested I do a mock session in one of the vacant classrooms before the final day. He also made it a point to ask me a number of germane *and* irrelevant questions, stop me in the middle of my sentences, and yes, hoot at me too! He was creating the worst possible audience scenario. I am glad he did for it prepared me for anything the real audience could have come up with. The practice run had an immense bearing on the actual presentation. I was much more comfortable and it also helped me edit my material to keep within the allotted time. I learnt a useful lesson from this experience. Practice goes a long way in easing the tension of speaking.

After my graduation as an engineer, I started teaching undergraduates. Every class and each exposure to a hall full of students helped me hone my skills of communication. Besides, I realize now that deep down I love speaking. This seems to have motivated me further, over the years, to remove the rough edges and make my speeches as flawless as possible.

After a brief break, during which I reared my first born, I came back to yet another powerful set of experiences: this time in the role of a Management Consultant and Trainer. From selling my training packages to actually conducting workshops, I had to speak constantly. I never stopped working on my personal style, material and resources, to make my presentations audience-friendly.

There is a saying, that when you prepare well, you begin well. And well begun is half done. How true! Consistent and continuous preparation and planning have worked wonders for my talks. If I once believed that there existed born speakers, my own experiences have proved me wrong! Today I believe that *good speakers are a creation of commitment, constant hard work and a willingness to evolve and change.*

Now I have come to a stage where I am willing to speak anytime, anywhere, and on any occasion! This hasn't happened overnight. I have worked towards this and am still working on further improving my skills.

After every 'Presentation Skills' or 'Communication' workshop that I conduct, my belief is reinforced. Speaking is truly a skill that can be learnt by everyone provided the individual is willing to invest the time and energy to master it.

As a reader, you could start reading the book wherever you like. But I would recommend that you go through the chapters systematically from the beginning, making mental notes of the points to be remembered. There is a well-structured sequence that I have constructed following which would prove beneficial.

The very fact that you have picked up this book hints at your desire of being an effective communicator. I hope you benefit from this book and are able to make an impact as a public speaker.

When I first thought of writing a book on Presentation Skills, my immediate reaction was: *Why another book?* There is already so much material available in the area of presentation skills, that I wondered and asked myself how my book would be different. Was I writing just because I had to or because I was genuinely trying to satisfy some need I had noticed in people seeking to perfect the art of public speaking? It didn't take me long to answer that. After a couple of days of quiet contemplation, I *knew* how my book would be useful *and* different at the same time.

I have always liked reading self-help books presented in a question-and-answer format. I therefore chose to adhere to a similar pattern for a major 'part of the book. Such a format is not only reader-friendly but helps answer specific concerns. The experience of conducting regular training workshops on presentation skills over the past ten years helped me enumerate common questions asked by participants. I then went a step further and collected information from various professionals about *their* apprehensions of public speaking. All this helped me address some of the pressing concerns of public speakers.

I do realize that readers of this book will be at different levels of proficiency as speakers and I have, accordingly, tried to cater to various needs. Starting from the basics, or *ab initio* as some would say, always helps. Therefore, Part One of this book highlights the basics of effective communication and spells out in detail the contents of the toolkit an effective speaker requires.

Part Two, which in fact forms the bulk of the book, deals with the various aspects that make up a presentation, from preparation to delivery.

Though the basics of good communication do not really change, presentations made by different professionals do differ. I haven't come across any book which deals separately with presentations made by different professionals. This is precisely what I have detailed in Part Three. I have discussed, *inter alia*, presentations made by a television host, an advertising executive, and a sales professional. This part of the book helps draw out the finer, distinguishing aspects of various types of presentations. Besides, *this* is what makes my book really different!

Savita Bhan Wakhlu

ACKNOWLEDGEMENTS

The seed of this book was planted in my mind almost five years back. The very idea of writing about something so close to my heart, and around which my work revolved, had me elated. But when I actually started penning down my thoughts, my motivation levels dropped. I realized that writing a book was not easy. I persisted, however. Progress was slow, more so because I had little time left after my consulting and training assignments coupled with the responsibilities of managing and running a home. Looking back, I am deeply aware that this book would not have been written at all had it not been for some very special people. Every project a person undertakes invariably involves the assistance of some others. To that extent even writing a book is the result of team effort.

One person who was keen to see my book written as early as possible, was my husband *Bharat*. My sincere gratitude goes to him for his constant prodding and affectionate nudging (or should that be nagging?). I must admit that I did not much appreciate his comments then, as it was rather annoying to be reminded that I was not putting in enough effort to complete the draft. Thankfully, there is no rancour now!

I was fortunate that my early education was at a well-established convent school and for this, and for the wonderful upbringing I've had, I am ever so grateful to my parents, *Sheila* and *Brijmohan Bhan*. I vividly remember the many occasions when I would switch from speaking my mother tongue *Kashmiri* to *English* in my conversations at home; my parents would always encourage me and appreciate my initiative to hone my English speaking skills.

I finally got down to serious and committed writing during the last year and a half. My deep appreciation goes to my secretary, *Sachi Das*. Her presence, and her eagerness to move on to the next chapter after we had finished one, galvanized my thought process. Her efficiency on the computer helped my ideas take shape.

In our family the writing bug seems to have bitten almost everyone. My parents-in-law, *Kshema* and *Omkar* have authored novels, and books on the politics of Kashmir and on Management. So has my brother-in-law *Arun*. Whenever I'd meet them, they would enquire lovingly about the progress of my book. This itself was sufficient inspiration and encouragement. Thank you for being the way you are.

I cannot put in words the immense patience shown by *Ranjan Kaul*, General Manager, Response Books. His regular e-mails, which would convey his desire to see me successfully through with my project, as well as the feedback he sent on the manuscript, proved extremely helpful in planning and writing the book. He has been a pillar of extraordinary support and guidance, applying just the right kind of pressure to get me going. I am immensely grateful to him.

I also want to express my gratefulness to all my students at XLRI, Jamshedpur, and the many participants of my training programmes who, by virtue of their genuine concerns and queries about speaking in public, gave me an opportunity to further explore this territory.

A lot of value has been added to the book by the excellent sketches of *Debasish Deb*, the Resident Artist of the *Telegraph*. His sketches, which we became familiar with while he'd illustrate our fortnightly column in the Jamshedpur edition of the *Telegraph*, are very impressive. I couldn't have asked for a better illustrator for this book. I am particularly thankful to Debasish for his co-operation and support.

My list of acknowledgements would be incomplete without mentioning the splendid job done by *Sangeeta Goswami*, Editor, Response Books. Her editorial approach has made the book more readable and crisp. *Richard Brown*, also of Response Books, checked the proofs and has helped to weed out typographical errors.

SBW

Part One

COMMUNICATION: THE FOUNDATION

1

INTRODUCTION

The term 'communication'—haven't you heard the word often before? It means different things to different people. What the term means to you could be different from what it means to somebody else. Irrespective of what meaning you assign to this term, you cannot doubt its importance in everyday life.

From the moment a baby is born, before it has learned to speak, it starts communicating with people around. And, people attending to it—the mother, grandparents or even a nanny—are soon able to interpret what the infant is trying to convey. As we grow, we learn the wonderful ability to use appropriate words and phrases to convey our ideas and feelings. We get better and better at the art as we understand the nuances of the language we have learned, and use the subtle differences between words to convey our views with greater

effectiveness. Unlike the rest of the animal world, where 'fight' and 'flight' are the only known responses, the evolved homo sapien has the unique quality of demonstrating verbal fluency.

There is no doubt that we all need to communicate. Not just on a one-to-one basis, but more importantly, in situations where you need to inspire action and get results. The ability to communicate well is a skill which can be enhanced by effort and practice.

The practice of management, which involves such aspects as planning, organizing, achieving results and motivating people, hinges upon communication. Managers at the top rung of an organization usually define the strategic objectives of their enterprise. These objectives are then broken down into specific, time-bound goals that each department or division has to achieve. Managers at different levels further translate these goals into specific task plans. The responsibility of accomplishing these plans rests with the individual members of the group.

All this is just not possible without ensuring the complete involvement of each member. To enlist their support, it is imperative that senior managers effectively communicate to them their vision of the desired future. This is where communication assumes an important role.

Typically, managers do not use the vehicle of communication only to inform or instruct. There are several other equally important reasons why they need to communicate effectively:

- Managers are leaders, and one of their vital tasks is to energize their people. Communication makes that possible.

SUPERIOR

CUSTOMER

MANAGER
EXECUTIVE

SUPPLIER

COLLEAGUE/SUBORDINATE

EFFECTIVE
COMMUNICATION

- Managers are expected to create harmony and ensure teamwork. Communication, by virtue of being a two-way process, helps to build effective relationships. For this, however, one has to be aware of the different barriers that can block the communication process.

- All effective, change-ready, learning organizations have to continuously improve and adopt new procedures and processes. It is only through the process of communication that the benefits of change can be conveyed, and thereafter effectively introduced. Communication can also help minimize the negative reactions to change and ensure the support of the people in the change effort.

- Good organizations exist in harmony with the outside world. This implies managing relationships with the stakeholders, such as customers, suppliers, vendors, and the public. Keeping open channels of communication is the only effective way in which this can be done.

- Managers represent their companies across local and often global markets. In such a role they need to interact a great deal with all kinds of people. Mastering the art of presentation skills, or public speaking, is absolutely essential for this.

To sum up, communication is at the heart of making 'connections'—establishing links with people, building rapport, and forging alliances and partnerships that are harmonious and fruitful. Presentation skills, which are a subset of all the abilities available to us as communicators, are an integral part of this larger process. And mastering them is, therefore, an essential prerequisite for success.

2

THE COMMUNICATION PROCESS: VERBAL AND NON-VERBAL

How well we communicate is determined not by how well we say things, but how well we are understood.
　　　　　　　　　　　　　　　—Andrew S. Grove, former CEO
　　　　　　　　　　　　　　　　　　　　Intel Corporation

Before you embark on improving your communication ability, you need to understand the *process* of communication. Once you are completely aware of the process, you will be in a better position to surmount the barriers that hinder communication. We all need to increase the chances of people understanding us; after all it feels good to be correctly understood! As Andrew Grove has aptly pointed out, being understood is the cornerstone of communication.

The communication process requires both a sender and a receiver. The sender could want to transmit an idea, a feeling or some information. The message could be a simple greeting or a very complex technical proposal. In either case, the sender would need to have a clear picture in mind of what she wants to get across. The clearer this image, the better the communication is likely to be.

Before beginning the actual communication, you need to encode the image you have in mind. There are a variety of 'codes' available to you: words, symbols or other gestures. The challenge for a speaker is to learn the use of the most appropriate 'code' to transmit ideas to the listener. The next step is when the listener receives the encoded message. The degree of understanding demonstrated by the receiver is a function of how 'correctly' the listener perceives and interprets the incoming communication.

This process of reconverting the message into an idea or image by the receiver is called decoding. The loop of the *coding-communicating-decoding-understanding* cycle is closed when

THE PROCESS OF COMMUNICATION

the receiver provides feedback to the sender, thereby demonstrating whether the understanding of the idea was as intended.

The media used for communication could vary from a written letter or email to a face-to-face dialogue. The selection of the right medium is obviously your responsibility as the sender, and you should be guided by the receiver's convenience and level of comfort with it. You need to be sufficiently sensitive to be able to 'tune-in' to the wavelength of the receiver and choose the most appropriate medium. It would be ridiculous to write a letter to one who is illiterate, just as it would be equally out of place to speak to someone in a language she doesn't know!

To be an effective communicator, you need to be sensitive to the likely impediments in the essential communication process and try to minimize them as far as possible.

THE ELEMENTS OF VERBAL COMMUNICATION

To be able to enhance your communication ability as a speaker, you need to first understand the elements involved in effective verbal communication. This is a sequence of a few vital elements, all of which contribute to the *gestalt* of effective communication and understanding. Ignoring any of these elements can prove costly and as a conscientious speaker you can ill afford that!

As stated earlier, all verbal communication begins with ideas or thoughts that you might want to convey. You will have to encode your thoughts suitably in order to enhance comprehension by others. This requires that you choose the most appropriate language and words that you think will help in getting your message across. It is equally important to structure and sequence your ideas in a systematic manner. The final act of delivering the message involves the effective use of your voice in the process of transmission. Besides, mastering the non-verbal aspects of communication is equally vital (more about this later in the chapter). The process of communication is complete only when the feedback from the listener is obtained and it is confirmed that the message has been received as intended.

To recap, the elements of effective verbal communication can be listed as follows:

- Framing the idea/thought/image in your mind.
- Encoding the idea into suitable language and words.
- Sequencing and structuring the content.
- Delivering or expressing the encoded ideas through speech.
- Receiving feedback from the listener/s.

Words for Maximum Impact

The same thing can be said in a variety of ways depending on your choice and usage of words. The main difference between an ordinary speech and an excellent one is language. Packaging your ideas by choosing words carefully, helps you reach out to your listeners in the most effective way.

Fredrick Beuchner, a scintillating speaker and writer says: *'words have colour, depth, texture of their own, and power to evoke vastly more than they mean; words can be used to make things clear, make things vivid, make things interesting, and make things happen inside the one who reads them or hears them.'*

A few suggestions for improving your use of language are:

◆ Use the Language with Care
Speakers often misuse the language by resorting to what Edwin Newman called 'bloating' i.e., the addition of unnecessary, redundant words to express an idea. A few examples are phrases like *most unique, totally free, two-way communication,* and *foreign imports.* You can easily make do with a single word in these cases. Another habit that speakers develop is the use of jargon. Jargon consists of technical terms and specific terminology associated with a particular profession or business which only those within the profession are adept at understanding.

Some examples from the internet world are B2B (Business to Business), P2P (Peer to Peer and Pace to Profit) and ICQ (I Seek You—the well-known chat system). Such usage tends to complicate our speech unnecessarily.

We often take refuge in clichés. Hearing and reading them often, we involuntarily pick up their use. A few examples are: 'I beg to submit', 'for your kind information', 'for all practical purposes', etc. Communicating to express means making the language simple.

◆ Go for the Active Voice

Choose the active voice over the passive. It is more direct and much more clearly understood. 'It has been seen' should be substituted by 'I saw'. It makes more of an impact as you then appear to be taking responsibility for what you are saying. This is something every audience appreciates.

◆ Use Words that Communicate Feelings

Each of us thinks and feels. And, if you are in the business of speaking, you can use these attributes to reach out to people by choosing words and phrases that appeal to the listeners' physical senses and feelings. While collecting relief for flood victims, for example, a phrase like 'imagine yourself going through this calamity . . .' would be quite appropriate to elicit a response.

> When *Abraham Lincoln* delivered the Gettysburg address, many listeners wept. It is not always necessary to make people cry in order to communicate effectively! You could use other emotions as effectively.

> *Gorgias*, a Greek who lived in the fourth century BC, was renowned in Athens for using language so beautiful that people thought it was magic. Three centuries earlier, *Archie Lochus*, another master of words, had a reputation for using caustic phrases. The story goes that his in-laws were so upset by his words one day that they killed themselves. You need not make your words so pungent, but adding power and punch are beneficial.

◆ Avoid Modifiers

Powerful speakers use fewer phrases that can weaken their language. A few examples are: *perhaps, may be, could be,* and *should be.* Avoid saying 'you could get the material' when you can say 'you will get the material'. Social scientists at *Duke University* (Leeds, 1990) have been able to pinpoint a specific pattern that identifies powerless speech. Research conducted here confirms that intensifiers like *very, definitely, surely* do just the opposite of what one expects them to do. They weaken the descriptive adjective that follows by not letting it stand on its own. For example 'this package is unique' is far superior to 'this package is very unique'.

◆ Use Metaphors to Your Advantage

When words are chosen with care, vivid images are created that can make a speech memorable and render it a part of history. *Martin Luther King Jr.* was a master of the metaphor as is evident in his famous speech, 'I Have a Dream',

> *One hundred years later, the life of the Negro is still sadly crippled by the manacles of segregation and the chains of discrimination. One hundred years later, the Negro lives on a lonely island of poverty in the midst of a vast ocean of material prosperity . . . .*

The use of the simile offers a technique with which to compare ideas using the words *like* and *as.* When I talk about Presentation Skills, I use many similes. Many of them are thought of there and then. For instance, the ability to communicate well is like ferrying passengers across a river safely to the other bank. One must be able to think on one's feet. Moreover, an open mind, and the ability to view situations and events from various perspectives, can help you think of appropriate similies.

◆ Use Words which Come Easily to You

Contrived language loses its impact. You don't have to use complicated words to be an effective speaker. Use language you are comfortable with, and use it as best as you can.

If you do want to use a new word, then you have to familiarise yourself with it by knowing its precise meaning and pronunciation. Consistent use of new words can help you use them with ease.

If you want your speech to rise above the ordinary, you have to take special care while choosing your words. With practice, and a desire to improve your style, you can positively substitute the mundane by the interesting.

NON-VERBAL COMMUNICATION

It may sound absurd, but it is a fact that a large contribution to your message comes from what you don't actually say. The way you stand, the gestures you use and your facial expressions are all integral parts of communication. How many times have you heard a speaker on a topic that is of interest to you, but you are somehow unable to give it all your attention? The problem could lie in the style of the presenter and the way she comes across.

You might think there could be no problem once you have prepared and structured your presentation. You might even believe that all you have to do is stand up and speak. To some extent you are right. Thorough preparation, along with a logical structure, do go a long way in getting a speaker ready. But, if you have not paid any heed to your delivery style, you could be creating an insurmountable barrier in your communication. If your non-verbal, body signals are not synchronized with your words, your message will not have the desired impact. An effective speaker knows he must master the verbal part of his presentation, but knows he cannot neglect the non-verbal component either.

A few vital areas that you need to work upon to improve your body language are given below.

Eye Contact

The first 'contact' you make with your audience, well before you start speaking, is with your eyes. Your initial glance conveys either your level of comfort and confidence or your discomfort and nervousness. Your eyes not only signal but also receive messages. You can discern from the audience's looks and postures their state of mind. Just as they are constantly gauging you through your movements, you too need to make an assessment and start forging a positive, friendly relationship with them.

Maintaining consistent and healthy eye contact is necessary. Many speakers take refuge by totally avoiding eye contact, looking instead at the ceiling, the floor, the lectern and even the walls. Though it is difficult to make eye contact with an unfamiliar or new group, it is essential and needs to be practised. The hesitation arises because of the nervousness that most speakers experience while speaking. It may sound paradoxical, but maintaining eye contact with the audience is one of the antidotes for such anxiety.

When you enter the room or the venue, look at your entire audience in one quick sweep. Then take a few seconds to look

BE IN CONSTANT TOUCH THROUGH EYE CONTACT

around the room and 'your space'—the area from where you will be addressing the group. Making yourself comfortable before you start speaking is essential. It conveys a positive message about your condition and puts the audience at ease too. Adequate eye contact coupled with a friendly smile further helps build rapport with your audience.

In the course of your presentation you might use index cards which highlight your speaking points or ideas, or you might read from a prepared script. In either case, spending time looking at the people listening to you is necessary. Too often, speakers forget this and are guilty of constantly looking down at their notes. Ideally, you should run your eyes over the audience at intervals. Another point to remember is that you should avoid developing a 'bias' towards a certain side of the room or auditorium. If you are speaking to an auditorium full of people you could try and glance at most of the listeners by drawing an imaginary **M** or a **W** across the hall with your eyes.

Body Posture

The way you sit or stand also conveys a message to those watching. A sloppy posture communicates a lack of confidence. The simple rules which, if followed, never fail to send a positive signal are:

- Be as relaxed as possible.
- Stand straight so that your body is erect. Take care, however, that the process of standing upright is not transformed into stiffness.
- Your body weight should be balanced equally on both your feet.
- Avoid leaning on the lectern or a side wall.
- Avoid rocking movements. Constant shifting can distract your audience.
- Place your notes or index cards at an angle where you don't have to slouch in order to read. Precious eye contact is lost when you have to bend to consult your notes. Decide where you want your notes to be placed for easy reading.

FIG LEAF

PARADE REST

LECTERN FIXATION

POCKET JINGLE

Gestures

In my training workshops on presentation skills, I am often faced with a query from participants wanting to know what they should do with their hands while speaking. While speaking to groups of people, our hands often seem to be an encumbrance rather than an asset. I have realized over the years that the gestures of effective speakers—people who are clear about their message and in tune with their audience—automatically reinforce what they are saying. Gestures are the natural movements of our upper limbs, including our hands, head and shoulders. Often, because of nervousness and anxiety, you may unconsciously lock your arms against your body, sending the wrong signal. Human beings are so used to making gestures, easily and unknowingly, in their day-to-day conversations that they are not aware how much their hands and arms come into play when they talk. The same sort of natural spontaneity should occur in front of an audience since speaking in public is, in a sense, akin to talking to an extended circle of people.

Remember your hands will take care of themselves and augment your presentation with the appropriate gestures, as long as you don't do the following:

- Grab the lectern for support.
- Keep your hands in your pockets all through your presentation.
- Clutch your arms and lock them against your chest.
- Fiddle with your jewellery or any other prop.

You could use natural gestures to communicate shapes, sizes, numbers or even point at a flip chart or board to highlight a point.

I have seen speakers in my training sessions using pronounced hand and arm movements to prove their point. Unfortunately, unnatural gestures work against you and cause a certain degree of distraction instead. The easiest thing would be to let your hands hang by your side. Another simple technique is to engage your hands, without undue force or

SHOWING A SHAPE

EMPHASIZE

ENUMERATE

POINTING

pressure, and keep them at the diaphragm level. When you want to use them for a particular gesture, unlock them, use them and then go back to your original position. Doesn't that sound simple enough?

Facial Expressions

A warm, friendly speaker is always welcome and eagerly heard. Your smile puts you and the audience at ease. Smiling helps you loosen and relax your facial muscles. You even look better when you smile. Try it in front of your mirror and you will not disagree. A grim look will always alienate you from your listeners.

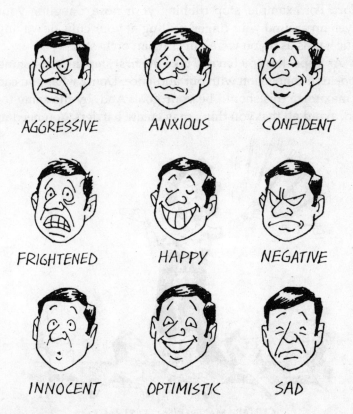

AGGRESSIVE   ANXIOUS   CONFIDENT

FRIGHTENED   HAPPY   NEGATIVE

INNOCENT   OPTIMISTIC   SAD

As a frequent presenter myself and through interactions with my audience I realize that we smile much less than normal when addressing groups of people. In fact, whenever I am faced with a stern, serious looking participant, I have to remind him/her to smile more often. This has a positive effect on the person and substantially reduces his/her anxiety.

Distracting Mannerisms

Beware of any distracting mannerism that can divert the attention of your audience. Nervous mannerisms can be controlled provided one is aware of these and sincere about reducing their occurrence. Once you have identified such a mannerism, you can go about reducing it with a conscious effort. For example, stop rubbing your nose, dangling your keychain around your finger, pulling at your cuffs or waving your hands as if you were directing an orchestra.

As a speaker you have to take the first step in establishing a positive connection with our audience. Doing what you can to maximize this should be your goal. And, by the same token, avoid all that you think may create barriers. You need to

CERTAIN MANNERISMS DISTRACT

bridge the gap with the audience. For example, standing behind a lectern immediately isolates you from them. You will need to make the extra effort to connect with the group.

Communication can be either *one-to-one* or *one-to-a-group*. The basics of effective communication remain the same in either situation. But somehow it seems easier to convey a message to an individual rather than to a group. This isn't surprising, considering that *one-to-one* communication is what we start off with as children. Speaking to a group becomes a need as we enter into roles that require communicating with larger audiences.

The fears and concerns of speaking to a group could be many. Typically, these revolve around how one needs to handle 'difficult' listeners, how one can remember the 'material' one has chosen to convey, or even how to select the right kind of material for a certain presentation. All these are genuine concerns that good speakers have learned how to surmount. Explained in this book are a number of proven techniques that help one tide over these concerns. Applying these techniques will enable you to master the skill of speaking in public **without** anxiety.

Part Two

THE A–Z OF MAKING
PRESENTATIONS

3

SPEAKING IN PUBLIC

The magical gift of speech has been bestowed only on human beings. It is a quality that can be used by an individual to influence people. People skilled in the art of effective speaking are able to touch the lives of thousands. There is immense power in words and more so when they are used well. Good speakers can move audiences and often, entire nations as well.

Despite being closely related to our existence, speaking in public does cause a great degree of anxiety and apprehension to the speaker. Speaking one-to-one seems to occur quite naturally and spontaneously. But the moment one is asked to address a group of people or present ideas at meetings, team briefings, training programmes or in a setting that calls for a formal presentation, one often hesitates. This hesitation arises either because the prospective speaker has never spoken

before a large group or because the skills needed to do so have not been consciously developed.

Most managers are required, at least occasionally, to address groups of people and their ability to present ideas effectively is being increasingly assessed as a desirable attribute. Many managers try to avoid situations where they have to indulge in 'public speaking'. Though the phrase may conjure up images of a politician canvassing at election time or an expert addressing a large audience at a seminar, it is not only these big events that constitute public speaking. Even day-to-day interactions or speeches that form a part of the typical working day of an executive, fall under this gamut.

Research has shown that managers who lack the ability to communicate effectively acquire a reputation of being dull, unsure of themselves and weak at managing. In fact, illustrative of this is the case of two executives I know who were in a large manufacturing firm. One of them, having mastered the art of public speaking, effectively communicated with her team and external agencies. The other was a comparatively dull and a diffident speaker. After a decade, the former was Vice President of her division while the latter had stagnated at the level of manager. Both of them may have been equally capable to begin with, but then one had a distinctive edge over the other. If you do not sharpen your speaking skills and use them to your advantage, you will soon find yourself overtaken in the organization.

Public speaking, thankfully, is a learnable skill. Practice, after mastering the techniques involved, almost always assures success. Somebody once asked a woodcarver, 'How do you carve such magnificent elephants from a block of wood?' 'Simple', the woodcarver replied, 'you chip away what does not look like an elephant'.

This is also true of speaking in public. You need to work constantly on your style. Speaking well in public will follow from the painstaking removal of weaknesses or the redundant from your repertoire of speech-related abilities. Learning how to speak effectively is a continuous process. Being born with the 'gift of the gab' or being a 'born speaker' are myths. You have to strive towards your goal. It is possible, albeit difficult and painstaking at times, to master the skill of speaking in public.

All of us possess the potential to turn into effective speakers and presenters. All it needs is an understanding of the factors that influence speaking, a burning desire to learn and master the elements that constitute good public speaking and developing the courage and confidence to deliver an effective speech. It may seem like an arduous task, but let me assure you that it is not! Many before have done it with ease and so can you!

Before we move on further, I suggest you evaluate the current level of your presentation effectiveness. For that you will need to honestly fill in the questionnaire given below. After completing the questionnaire, you can use the scoring sheet given at the end of the chapter to make an assessment of your skills. Irrespective of your score, you will get a feel of the factors that need to be considered while speaking.

4

EVALUATION OF YOUR PRESENTATION SKILLS

Fill in the questionnaire given below. Your answers will be based on your current ability to make presentations. You can encircle the number which is closest to your present level.

5 = Always, 4 = Frequently, 3 = Sometimes, 2 = Occasionally, 1 = Never

1. My main aim in making a   5   4   3   2   1
   presentation is to get my
   message across.

2. I specifically define my objectives before the presentation.

    5   4   3   2   1

3. I analyze the needs, the composition and the limitations of my audience.

    5   4   3   2   1

4. I brainstorm for ideas in order to build my presentation.

    5   4   3   2   1

5. I work on the introduction of my talk to make it catchy, and to give the audience the necessary opening information.

    5   4   3   2   1

6. I develop the conclusion and, if needed, incorporate the 'call to action' (follow-up action) statement.

    5   4   3   2   1

7. The visual aids I use are simple, legible, carefully prepared and have the desired impact.

    5   4   3   2   1

8. I use visual aids to support my verbal message, not to replace it.

    5   4   3   2   1

9. I rehearse what I am going to present and do on the final day.

    5   4   3   2   1

10. I do not rehearse my speech by learning each word. I remember the main ideas, instead.

    5   4   3   2   1

11. My notes highlight just   5   4   3   2   1
    the main/key ideas so
    that I do not need to
    read from them directly.

12. I work systematically on my   5   4   3   2   1
    symptoms of nervousness and
    take appropriate remedial actions.

13. I maintain a consistent,   5   4   3   2   1
    healthy eye contact with
    the audience.

14. I am enthusiastic while   5   4   3   2   1
    communicating my ideas.

15. I anticipate questions and   5   4   3   2   1
    prepare accordingly.

16. In case I do not know the   5   4   3   2   1
    answer to any question, I
    admit it honestly.

17. My gestures are natural   5   4   3   2   1
    and help me in getting my
    message across.

18. I work on my vocal   5   4   3   2   1
    attributes such as clarity,
    volume and tone.

19. I arrange the seating   5   4   3   2   1
    of the audience, if possible,
    in a manner that best suits
    my presentation. I also check
    the set-up of the room and the
    equipment I shall be using.

20. I keep in mind the time factor   5   4   3   2   1
    while making my presentation
    including the time of day and
    the total time available.

Scoring—*Add your scores for the above questions*

80–100   Well done. You have grasped the nuances of making an effective presentation. This book will help you confirm the ideas you believe in.

60–80   You are close to the target of becoming an effective speaker. Go through the book to hone your skills further.

40–60   You have to work hard to master the ABCs of a good presentation. It is not tough but it takes practice and patience.

20–40   You have a long way to go. Don't lose heart. It is only a question of increasing your awareness, motivating yourself and utilising the inputs this book provides. You will reach your destination sooner than you think.

20   You may have to go through this book from cover to cover to attune yourself to the art of speaking. You *can* do it, as have many others before you.

After the evaluation some of you may be delighted with your scores and some disappointed. The latter need to bolster their courage and believe that they too will taste success soon. However, to see tangible improvements in your skill of speaking demands commitment and action.

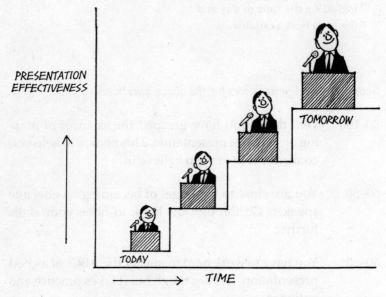

PRESENTATION
EFFECTIVENESS

TOMORROW

TODAY

TIME

IMPROVEMENT IN SPEAKING SKILLS WITH TIME

5

TAKING CARE OF YOUR NERVES

If somebody told you he did not feel nervous while addressing a group of people, you would be advised to take it with a pinch of salt! What you experience in front of an audience is what every other speaker experiences. While training hundreds of participants in public speaking, I have rarely met an individual who didn't complain of anxiety and stress when asked to speak in public. The degree of uneasiness may vary among speakers. A lot depends on how frequently you get to face large gatherings in the course of your work. The more experience you gain, the more confident you feel.

While conducting a course on 'public speaking' at a management school, I once had a student who always avoided making her presentation. I tried to give her as many opportunities as I could, to speak, so that she could get over her fear.

And remember, she only had to speak in front of her class fellows, most of whom she knew well. Yet, she never obliged! Her grade was obviously affected, but I was more concerned about something else. She was leaving the institute with the false notion that she could not speak in public. Not surprisingly, her written assignments were very well drafted and presented. So, the problem wasn't a lack of ideas or insufficient control over the English language. It was just a case of what we refer to as 'stage anxiety'. It sounds unbelievable, but people are really quite scared of speaking in public. The *Chicago Tribune* (Whalen 65) undertook a survey some years back to find out what people were most afraid of. The compiled answers go on to list the most frequently stated fears in descending order:

Rank	Fear
1	Public Speaking
2	Heights
3	Insects
4	Financial difficulties
5	Deep water
6	Illness
7	Death
8	Flying (or crashing)

The fear of speaking can manifest itself in a variety of symptoms. You could experience one, or a combination of unpleasant feelings and sensations. You might be afflicted with a discernible pounding of your heart, sweaty palms, queasy intestines, a dry mouth, stiff muscles in the neck, and even the blanking out of thought. And this list is in no way exhaustive!

It would be good to begin with an understanding of what makes us so fearful of speaking in public. It becomes easier then to work on the erroneous attitudes and thinking patterns that underlie such fears. By dealing with our thoughts and attitudes we can, thus, reduce our stress symptoms considerably.

An exercise I use frequently in my speaking skill workshops is to ask participants to jot down their worst fears vis-à-

vis public speaking. The reasons stated are invariably diverse but I have classified them into four broad categories. These are:

- The fear of the audience itself.
- Fears related to the material/content.
- Fears relating to the use and handling of presentation resources.
- Fears about one's own abilities.

We need to look at each category in some detail.

Fear of the Audience

If you were speaking in an empty room, I can assure you that you wouldn't feel nervous at all! It is the audience that makes speakers tense. It's only natural, and needs to be accepted.

Typical concerns of the speaker regarding the audience include:

- They are more intelligent than I am and know more about the topic.
- Will they understand me?
- They may get bored and prove disinterested.
- They may already have heard what I am going to say.
- They may ask questions that I have no answers for.
- They will observe me so carefully that it will make me uncomfortable.

A few helpful suggestions to reduce audience related fears are explained below.

◆ Know Your Audience

Never take your audience for granted. Having no regard for what they might like to listen to is cruel. If you want to get your message across effectively, you must express it in a way that appeals to your audience. It always helps to search for answers to questions such as, 'who will be there?', 'how many

TARGETING YOUR AUDIENCE

will be present?, and 'what are their expectations from the talk?'. The more you know the audience, the more you can influence them by including in your speech all that is relevant.

You have to appreciate that an 'unknown' audience will only increase your anxiety and apprehension. Getting to know the audience builds understanding, trust and a sense of ease. Even under normal circumstances, the blood pressure of human beings is known to rise when they speak. Why make matters worse by keeping yourself in the dark about the audience?

You could garner information about your prospective listeners from the organizers of the function, the sponsor of the event or even from the agenda of the meeting.

If you want to capture the attention of your listeners then make sure what you say is relevant to them. Package it in a way that is easily understood and do not say or do anything that can offend or threaten them.

◆ See Your Audience as Your Ally

You could perceive the audience as your ally or your competitor. The choice you make determines the consequences. What you think of your listeners impacts your behaviour towards them. You send out subtle signals through your non-verbal communication as well as your choice of verbal cues. Respect your audience. Do not think of them as mere 'blobs' of flesh and blood without any intelligence. Building a rapport with them helps you remove the barriers that initially exist between speaker and audience.

◆ Remember, You are the Expert

If you find yourself speaking to people on a topic, you are obviously an expert in the area. You will undoubtedly know more than your audience if you have prepared well. Being sensitive towards your group's needs requires making your material user-friendly and easily understandable.

Even if the audience has some previous knowledge of the topic, a concern of many a speaker, the success of your speech depends on your presentation technique, the content and the overall delivery. How many times have you picked up books on the same topic and liked just one or two? The selection and sequencing of material in the book, its printing and appearance, and the author's personal style mark out a successful book. The same holds true for verbal presentations.

So, make the most of the opportunity you have been given, and deliver your piece in a professional way.

Fear Related to the Material/Content

Here, too, your fears could fall under a broad spectrum. Data that I have collected and organized reveals that material- or content-related apprehensions were voiced as follows:

- Is the material relevant to the group?
- Is the material adequate?
- Should I focus on the general ideas or delve deep into the content?
- What if they have already seen the material I intend using?
- Is the material understandable and coherent?
- Is it visually stimulating?

There could, of course, be other concerns. Let us see how we can tackle these.

First of all you could breathe a sigh of relief! After all, you are the only one who has control over your material. The more carefully you plan the content, in terms of the sequence and structure, the more confident you will feel. A few pointers in this direction are suggested below.

◆ Prepare Your Speech

Prior preparation is a major part of an effective presentation. It is essential to cull your material through research by consulting books, the internet, magazines/periodicals, videos or experts in the relevant area. You must rework your speech till you feel it is interesting enough and will benefit your audience.

♦ Organize Your Material

It is not just the collection of information that is important. It is equally necessary to structure and organize it systematically. (This will be covered in more detail in Chapter 7).

♦ Practice Helps

If you aren't a regular speaker, then you need to practice before you speak in public. Practice will help you perfect your skill. An additional benefit is that your comfort level will be enhanced. You could practice alone, in front of a mirror or with a few well-wishers/friends. If you have the time, and would not mind the experience, you could get yourself videotaped to gather first-hand feedback. This will also help you time your speech. You could then spruce it up if it is too long or add to it if necessary.

♦ Make the Material Appealing

People get bored if what they are exposed to is dull and lack-luster. A monotonous display of slides and the parroting of a script can prove tedious. You must plan the use of visuals to complement what you are saying.

♦ Rely on Index Cards

A grave concern for most of us while speaking in public is of forgetting what needs to be said next. A simple remedy for this so-called 'problem' is the use of index cards which highlight the key ideas of your talk in the right sequence. You can refer to these cards for help in triggering your memory. I would strongly recommend their usage.

Fears Relating to the Handling of Presentation Resources

Presentation resources is the term used to denote all that is used by a speaker to support his/her message. This includes audio-visual aids such as the overhead projector (OHP), the black- or whiteboard, the television, the video player, the computer/multimedia projector and even the handouts given to the audience.

A few of the apprehensions speakers share regarding these resources are:

- There could be an unscheduled power cut.
- The equipment being used might not run.
- The whole 'set-up' may be unfamiliar.

These are all genuine concerns. A few handy tips that will help you tide over these concerns are explained below.

◆ Familiarise Yourself with the 'Set-up'

Unknown events often create fear. Similarly, unfamiliar gadgets may induce in you a certain degree of nervousness and anxiety. The ideal antidote is to arrive early and get 'hands-on' experience with the aids and resources provided. You can always ask the coordinator/organizer of the event for guidance and assistance.

◆ Be Prepared for any Eventuality

You are your best visual aid. You will find this phrase repeated many times in this book but I believe it is vital. Once in a while you may be faced with disrupted power supply or a malfunctioning presentation device. Instead of creating a scene or getting unduly ruffled, it is essential to remain calm and poised. In such situations you must try and continue without having to pause for too long. In fact, being prepared for the worst is a good strategy. Imagine the old gurukul form of schooling in India where the gurus (teachers) taught under trees without any infrastructure. Yet, they inspired many and helped nurture wholistic individuals. So, if a similar condition arises when you discover that you have been left to your own devices, just use your ability and knowledge to communicate with the audience.

Fear About One's Own Abilities

This is a universal fear. You may lack confidence in your speaking abilities or be a victim of erroneous assumptions. Negative thoughts and beliefs are the first stumbling blocks to success in public speaking. 'I am not a born speaker' is one such self-limiting myth. Even good speakers have to continuously work on their skills. I have seen miracles happen in the course of my workshops on speaking. At first, many members of the group refuse to speak and even if they do, sound unsure and anxious. After a few sessions of sharing with them the techniques of effective presentations and some practice runs, the same shy and diffident speakers now refuse to stop!!

Some of the apprehensions that diffident speakers talk themselves into believing are:

- I may fail to deliver a good speech.
- My body language may either be too passive or too aggressive.
- My talk may be peppered with an overdose of common fillers such as 'you see', 'I mean', 'is it o.k.?', 'honestly', believe me' and others.
- I may overshoot the allotted time.
- I may not be able to cope with my anxiety symptoms.

All trepidation regarding handling yourself can be set aside by that great wonder drug 'confidence'. A few simple tips to boost your self-confidence are:

Think and talk positively about yourself and your speaking skills. The information you feed yourself often turns into reality. So make sure you start on a positive note by feeling good about yourself.

Separate your behaviour/actions from yourself. If on a certain occasion you do bungle with your content, data or any other aspect of your presentation, how does it really change you? Being able to distinguish between yourself as a person and your behaviour will prove very helpful. Mistakes can always be looked into and improved upon. But for your self-esteem to come crashing down because of a not-so-effective talk is totally uncalled for.

Learn to accept compliments as well as receive criticism. When you are praised for a job well done, thank the giver of the compliment without hesitation. Compliments enhance one's self-confidence. However, you must also remain calm in the face of critical remarks. Never let criticism overshadow you. It is only specific actions of yours that have been evaluated. Constructive feedback should be accepted in the right spirit and worked upon.

Assert yourself while sharing ideas or information. You might have to encounter a hostile or ill-mannered audience. At no point in time, however, should you let your self-value be diminished. Speak up in an assertive, straightforward and respectful manner.

Take the initiative. Step forward when you are invited to give a speech or make a presentation. Being proactive will only add a feather to your cap. You will also grow more confident.

Praise yourself. Do not minimize your accomplishments by trivializing them. Pat yourself on the back even if nobody else chooses to do so. Even if you have proposed a short vote of thanks, you deserve to be complimented. Many others cannot do as much.

In Chapter 8, '**The Final Act**', you will be reading about nervousness reducing techniques. Focussing on any one or a combination of techniques is bound to make you feel more at ease.

6

THE RELEVANCE OF PREPARATION

Whether speaking at a conference or a production meeting, preparation is essential. The best way to start is by asking yourself a few questions. The moment you have the answers to these relevant questions, you will be more in command of the situation and in a better position to enhance your speaking ability. Some of the answers will also aid you in making essential decisions before the event and thereby help you firm up what you are going to say and how you plan to say it. The basic tenet you could follow is to use Rudyard Kipling's six 'serving men'. These 'six men' are the simple questions, 'Why?' 'What?' 'Who?', 'Where?', 'When?' and 'How?'.

To begin with, you will have to determine *WHY* you are speaking at all. Thinking about this will help you define the objectives of your talk and give you a clear idea of what you

wish to accomplish through your presentation. You could be speaking to inform the audience, to persuade them, to teach or to entertain them. Referring back frequently to the purpose of your presentation will help you decide what to include and what not to. As a speaker, it is your responsibility to find out what the audience is going to gain from your talk. When you have assessed this concretely you will be in a better position to hold the attention of your audience. You may even be able to convince them and bring them around to your point of view. It is your clarity of purpose that helps the speech evolve positively. At the end of your presentation, the listener should not be left wondering about the purpose of your speech.

You must then move on to **WHAT** needs to be said. Deciding on this is the key to your speech. Selecting the content is a major task and is dependent on the objective of your presentation. Once that is specified, you will find it easier to decide on relevant subject matter. You will have to keep in mind the expectations of the people likely to listen to you. Sometimes, the time you have on hand for the speech can also influence what you say. Even the time allotted for preparation is crucial. If limited, then you may have to rely totally on your own ideas without having the opportunity to browse through books or the internet to decide on content.

Ascertaining **WHO** is likely to be listening to you remains the other vital input to be considered while planning a presentation. Knowing as much about the group as possible not just in terms of their average age, sex or background, but also how familiar they are with the topic and what exactly they expect from the interaction, helps immensely. The effective speaker spends a considerable amount of time designing the most appropriate presentation for his/her audience.

A couple of students from middle school, for example, were taken to visit a metallurgical laboratory. The group was excited and eagerly looking forward to the trip. Unfortunately for them, the trip started off with speaker after speaker presenting a chain of overhead transparencies relating to technical matters. The students were left dazed, not knowing what to make of it all. Finally one of the organizers realized that it would be more fruitful to take them around the laboratory for a live demonstration instead, and thus saved the day.

The next question you would need to answer is: **WHERE** is the presentation taking place?

Checking the venue where your presentation is due is very important. This may play a significant role in the quality of your delivery. You need to familiarize yourself with the place and be conversant with the layout of the room including the location of the electric controls. You may also need to check resources, like the audio-visual equipment, that you intend using. The seating arrangement should suit your presentation. Moreover, the ambience must be friendly, warm and comfortable.

You may also wish to know **WHEN** you are making your presentation. Though on the face of it this information may appear redundant, it is actually not. When you are asked to speak, the first thing you would want to know is when the event is taking place. This gives you an idea of how much time you have for preparation.

Another aspect you should consider is the time of day when you have to make your presentation. If you have any control over the schedule, try and choose an hour when your energy levels are high. Also, post-lunch sessions invariably induce sleep. Of course, you can tide over this difficulty by involving the audience as much as you can in your presentation as I have discovered while addressing many an afternoon training session. My track record so far, at keeping participants awake, has been rather good!

Adhering to the time schedule by planning the contents of the presentation is imperative. A speaker who sticks to his deadline communicates self-discipline and a healthy respect for his audience.

HOW should the presentation be made?

The actual dynamics of speaking, the 'how', will be dealt with in Chapter 8, 'The Final Act'.

The final act of making a presentation is akin to the visible, one-tenth portion of an iceberg! However, the success of your speech actually hinges on the not-so-apparent nine-tenths. This consists of your preparation. It is said that when you fail to prepare, you are preparing to fail!

Query

I have mastered the skills of oration. Do I also need to prepare?

Response

It is commendable that you are comfortable speaking in public. The ability to address groups of people with ease and confidence is a remarkable skill. But this skill alone is not enough to make a powerful presentation. If you want to sustain the group's interest and attention, you will need to offer more than your mere presence and oratory skills. The audience would want to take back with them something worthwhile and tangible. I therefore suggest that prior preparation would enhance your existing skills. Well-prepared speakers are concerned about the audience and a discerning audience, in turn, will appreciate this.

Query

In an attempt to convey to the audience as much as I can, I gather a lot of material for my presentation. How do I select thereafter?

Response

It is necessary to collect as much relevant information as you can. Once you are aware of the topic, you could start by noting down your initial thoughts on the subject. After this it is time to start collecting material from libraries, friends, books or the internet. It is better to be over-stocked than understocked. But what is essential after this is the screening process. Focussing on the main purpose of your talk will help you decide what to keep and what to remove.

Too much information in the form of facts, figures, data and lists unnecessarily burdens the listener. Moreover, these details can be located in the reference section of any library. What the audience is interested in is your understanding and interpretation of this information. Supporting your message with examples, anecdotes and illustrations is a better idea than just enumerating what you have compiled.

A rehearsal before the final presentation would help you decide what to discard and what to keep. Anything that is superfluous and does not add value to the presentation should be discarded. Select only those details that will be relevant to your particular audience. Put down the key ideas on index cards (also known as confidence cards). These will help trigger your memory. All this is undoubtedly hard work, but the exercise will ensure a good and thorough presentation.

Query

Is there anything 'external' to the task of preparation that needs to be considered?

Response

You are absolutely right—there are some 'external' aspects that should be kept in mind. I'm a great believer in checklists! You would need to pay attention to include in it the following:

◆ The Podium

It should be 2-3 sq.m in area, be at a height of about ½ m, and preferably be covered with a carpet or firm cloth to dampen the sound of footsteps.

◆ The Lectern

A desktop lectern is what is mostly available. If the lectern does not have a built-in light, avoid using an extra lamp; the light in the room should be sufficient. Lecterns can sometimes build a barrier between you and your audience.

◆ Overhead Projector (OHP)

A roll of transparency foil is better than loose transparencies as you can write directly on it. But the choice depends on your level of comfort and ease with either. Place the projector in a convenient place. If you are using loose sheets then arrange for a small table to keep them on. Keeping sufficient transparency pens handy is necessary.

◆ Pointer

There is a large variety available from the standard collapsible pointer to the laser pointer. If you don't have either, you could use a cutout in the shape of an arrow and place it on your slide to highlight the point you are making.

◆ Projector Screen

Place the screen at the most appropriate distance from the OHP. Do not make the room too dark especially if the OHP image is not sharp. Images should be clear and the text legible from across the room. The transparency should be projected in the centre of the screen.

◆ Microphone

Ideally, it is better to use a cordless microphone than a fixed one. If the group is small you may do away with the microphone altogether.

◆ Assistant/Technician

The presence of an individual who can assist you during your presentation can be a source of encouragement. If something goes wrong, or you suddenly require something, the assistant can always help.

◆ Lighting

If natural light in the room is insufficient, use artificial light. In such a case, make sure you familiarize yourself with the controls and the switchboard so that you can manoeuvre these on your own in case no help is available.

◆ Extra Room

A room close by which you and the participants can use for some group activity or just for a change from the routine of the presentation, can be helpful. Some venues have such provisions as part of their training/presentation infrastructure.

◆ Refreshments

Planning for and supervising the distribution of refreshments is a small activity but significant nevertheless. Soft-drinks/tea/coffee should be served at the right time and with efficiency.

◆ Seating Order

Participants should be as close to the speaker as possible. It is better to spread the group along the width of the room instead of the length. A 'U'- or 'V'-shaped seating arrangement is ideal for interactive presentations. But for larger groups and shorter presentations one could settle for the theatre style of seating. If you intend dividing the audience into formal discussion groups then you could seat them in small groups or clusters from the very beginning. If your group is small, do remove the extra chairs and place them at the back. Generally people have a tendency to go sit in the last rows. To avoid this, have someone direct the participants towards the front rows. Take

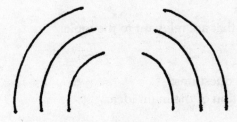

THEATRE STYLE

HORSE SHOE STYLE

MODIFIED THEATRE STYLE

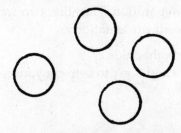

CABARET STYLE
FOR SMALL GROUPS

care that the chairs used are neither too comfortable (the audience may doze off!) nor too hard and difficult to sit on.

Query

I have noticed that presentations on the same topic, when delivered by different speakers, vary in their impact. How do some speakers manage to spark that interest while others are merely dull and boring?

Response

Presenters who are unable to express their ideas in the most effective way end up being tedious. In fact, the concentration level of individuals starts declining after the first 20 minutes or so. But a lot depends on what is said and more so, how it is said. Good presenters enrich their message with the help of:

- Analogies.
- Anecdotes.
- Examples that are relevant to the topic.
- Humour.
- Metaphors.
- Rhetorical questions.
- The repetition of the main idea.
- Statistics.

All these, used judiciously, could help build audience attention and interest. But their use has to be planned and this is also part of good preparation. The other two ways of enhancing the quality of your presentation are:

- Using visual and other aids.
- Using your voice and body to help get your message across forcefully.

Query

Could you elaborate on the use of analogies, anecdotes, humour, etc. needed to enhance ones presentation?

Response

I would like to suggest that you first identify what you are comfortable with and then go ahead and use it. If you are comfortable with quotations and have a rich fund available, you could intersperse your presentation with them. Personally, I enjoy using analogies. And, if I know my topic, the fertile soil of my thoughts often gives birth to analogies on the spot. Now, that is an analogy!

Let me give you a few examples to elaborate:

◆ Anecdote

It is a short narrative used to illustrate a point. It is sometimes humorous but not always. While speaking of the importance of time management, for example, you could say: 'When I conducted my first final year undergraduate class, I presented my material, hurriedly, in the first half hour itself while the actual duration of the class was a full hour'.

◆ Humour

Humour works with all groups and at all levels. But don't use it arbitrarily. It must be related either to the topic, the audience or the occasion. Also, never narrate a joke that is racist, sexist or that ridicules a religion or nation. To induce humour and creativity in a group, for example, you could say: 'imagine a hybrid between an animal and a vegetable!'

◆ Rhetorical Question

Questions are a powerful means of igniting interest and enthusiasm in a group. A rhetorical question has an obvious answer and you should know whether you want it answered by the listener or whether you will answer it yourself. In the latter case, you have to be prompt with the information. 'Are speaking skills learnable?' This could be a rhetorical question you pose to the audience in a talk on presentation skills. Questions of this kind are a simple method of gaining audience attention.

Whatever you use to support your message, plan, prepare and make yourself comfortable with it. Never try and adopt someone else's style.

Query

I have heard that the introduction to a presentation is called the 'prime time'. Why is this so?

Response

Powerful speakers start powerfully. The endeavour is to gain the audience's attention and interest the moment you walk onto the stage. Without attracting that attention, you will be unable to get your message across. The introduction to a presentation is indeed the prime time as that is when you establish rapport with your group. The introduction is also the 'bait' you use to motivate and persuade your audience to listen to you. In the introduction, you would tell them in brief what you intend telling them during the course of your presentation. You could start off with an anecdote, a joke, a quotation, a visually stimulating picture, or even an emphatic statement. This is not the time to offer apologies (for whatever reason), or embarrass your audience in any way. You are building a bridge during the first few minutes of your talk and it better be sturdy!

Query

Is the conclusion as important as the introduction?

Response

A strong conclusion is the climax to an effective presentation. It helps to arrange one's ideas in a series that culminate in a crescendo. The conclusion should definitely be as memorable as the introduction. The audience should leave with a good taste in their mouth. You could end by summarizing your key ideas, or wrap-up with a poem, an anecdote, a humorous piece or something that is visually appealing. Sometimes, while delivering a persuasive presentation, you may like to end your speech with a dynamic call to the audience urging them to take up a particular challenge.

Query

In some situations I have found that though a speaker is well-prepared and expresses himself/herself well, it is the speaker's overall appearance that puts the group off. I think the personality and the way the speaker is turned out also play a role in the communication process. Am I right?

Response

You are absolutely right. It is the combined effect of the ability of the speaker and his appearance that influences the group. When speakers dress appropriately, they show respect for the audience. You should look professional and be comfortable. Ideally, the kind of attire you choose would depend on the climate, the occasion and what looks good on you. The outfit should convey that you have taken care while selecting it. Avoid loud jewellery or other accessories that can distract your listener. You should dress in a subtle and sober manner in order to create a favourable impression.

7

ORGANIZING FOR A
SMOOTH FLOW OF IDEAS

The process of making a presentation begins with the preparation. But before you finally deliver the talk, you need to pay careful attention to the subject matter. Simply collecting material without developing a structure would be meaningless. Moreover, the audience would find it difficult to follow you. Make sure you are satisfied about the clarity of the message being delivered. An unstructured, rambling talk would be difficult to understand and concentrate on. You may be speaking on a relevant and interesting topic and your audience might be receptive and eager, but if you don't have a well-structured speech you will be forced to observe the ground slipping under your feet!

Proper organization of material helps save the audience from boredom. It is almost like carrying a train of passengers along the right track. Any unnecessary diversion brought about by the illogical or unsystematic flow of ideas, is bound to put your audience out of harmony with you. If you are aiming for resonance, spend adequate time planning, sequencing and structuring your material.

Query

How can I structure my presentation effectively?

Response

There are a couple of steps that you need to follow to develop a systematic presentation.

◆ Brainstorming

It is essential to 'brainstorm' and get all your thoughts and ideas about your presentation subject onto paper. Use separate sheets of paper/index cards for each idea. Brainstorming is the phase of ideation where the focus is on quantity not quality. Don't ever put a brake on the flow of ideas you are churning out, however divergent or creative. The process of screening begins only once you have a large number of ideas. Try and select between three and five main ideas resulting from your 'brainstorming' session.

◆ Identifying the Sub-points

Once you have identified the main points of your presentation, it is essential to develop supporting ideas. This may consist of explanations, data or further evidence to support your main ideas. Arrange the notes you have made to best complement the main ideas. You must keep referring back to the objective of your speech throughout this process as that would help you decide on the best way to append supporting ideas to the main ones. Clarity about the objective and a sound understanding of your audience and their needs will further illuminate your selection process.

◆ Structuring Your Message

You will need to weave your ideas into a short and simple message. 'KISS' is the well known acronym denoting the key to making an effective presentation—Keep It Short and Simple. It is something well worth remembering! Present your ideas in a natural and logical order. A suggestion that I personally find useful in this regard is to imagine myself a part of the audience.

Query

When we talk of structuring presentations are there any preferred or standard methods?

Response

You can present your speech in limitless ways provided it is understandable and audience-friendly. However, a few well-known and accepted methods are given below:

◆ Sequential Order

You could present events in the sequence they occur in. For example, **A** followed by **B**, and **B** followed by **C** is the order to follow while teaching a child the English alphabet. Similarly, if you are talking about some equipment, say, you will need to first define the equipment, then describe its construction and mechanics, after which you will need to focus on its working and uses. That would make it easy to understand. This is what sequential structuring is. A further subset of sequential order is the chronological sequence where the time/date factor becomes the focal point. A sequential train of thoughts is inherently logical and, therefore, simple for the audience to follow.

◆ Past, Present and Future

If you are delivering a talk on a topic where you need to compare a situation that is prevalent today with what was and what you expect it to be, then the 'past, present and future'

structure is useful. The CEO of a company, talking about the last few years of his company's performance and then sharing his vision of strategies for the future, could follow this method.

◆ Order of Importance

You may wish to sequence your material according to the relevance of the points that you wish to make—the important issues first followed by the trivial ones. For example, the principal of a college may wish to speak about the problem of indiscipline first and then take up regular academic information-sharing with students and faculty.

◆ Categories

This is useful when you lack a clear pattern of organization or your topic does not conform to a set procedure, process or timeframe. You can assign importance levels to the sub-topics you have chosen for your presentation. For example, if you are delivering a speech on 'The Art of Selling', you may categorize your material into the following sub-headings: Seller Personality, Understanding the Buyer, Sales Presentations, Handling Objections, and Closing the Sale. The categorical pattern works well when you are presenting new ideas or are developing your own framework.

◆ Order of Analysis

This is a very simple technique that helps create a sequence whereby the audience is 'hooked' to your speech. It is based on asking certain questions such as what? when? how? who? where? how many? how much? how often? who else? or any other query related to the topic, and analyzing the questions to organize your speech. It even gets your audience involved because many of the questions in their minds are being addressed. Whenever I address sessions on 'Communication Skills', I find it handy to use the order of analysis to explain the importance, benefits and process of communication.

◆ Rhetorical Questions

This method, in which your speech is organized around the answers to the rhetorical questions you select, can be very beneficial and thought provoking. It guarantees you audience participation and interest. But you have to decide whether you want to answer these questions yourself or would prefer to wait for the audience to reply. The danger is that the audience response could be totally divergent from what you were expecting and might jeopardize your presentation. For instance, while delivering a talk on 'Presentation Skills' you may like to start off by asking a rhetorical question such as, 'which is our worst fear?' You are probably expecting 'Public Speaking' as the response so that you could take off from there. But then the audience replies range from 'insects' to 'flying' So, be careful and try to remain in charge of the questions asked and answers given.

◆ Problem-Solving Formula

This pattern is commonly used in technical presentations but is effective for any talk where you need to demonstrate the current status or 'what is', the desired state or 'what ought to be', and how to bridge the gap between the two, or 'what needs to be done'. This pattern includes the following steps:

- Stating the problem and getting the audience to recognise the fact that problems exist and that something needs to be done about them.

- Offering solutions and informing the group how these would ensure that the problem is solved.

- Highlighting the reasons why you feel that the suggested solutions will work.

- Enlisting examples and evidence where such solutions have worked before.

- Motivating the audience to adopt the solutions offered by pointing towards the benefits that will accrue to them.

These are some of the preferred patterns of structuring your presentation. But as a speaker you are absolutely free to evolve your own structure by combining patterns that have been enumerated above. Just bear in mind that the sequence of your presentation follows a certain logic and is systematic and simple to grasp.

Query

Sometimes while speaking, I find myself waiting and wondering how I should move on and link the point I am making with the next one? Can this be avoided?

Response

We spend a lot of time and energy planning the introduction and conclusion of our speech. But we tend to neglect the main body of it. The movement from one idea to the next in the course of your speech should be smooth. When a train changes track, passengers don't mind as long as the change is subtle.

You could be stopping in-between because you haven't planned your shifts or transitions to connect the various points of your presentation. If you work on your transitions and decide beforehand how you would do this, the waiting periods may become less frequent and even less painful.

A few transition methods are given below.

◆ Physical Movement

A new idea can be introduced by changing your posture or position. You could sit if you have been standing all through. Moving away from the podium and speaking could serve the purpose too. If you have been moving back and forth, you may now decide to stand still to make a new point.

◆ Visual Aids

The use of visual aids is a powerful transition technique. When you start operating the resource that you have chosen, you are involving the listener in the message that you are conveying through the aid.

◆ Use of Linking Words

A simple method of connecting different ideas is the use of linking words such as *therefore, however, accordingly, in addition to, besides* and *lastly*. These words communicate change in the course of your speech and listener interest is revived.

◆ Posing Questions

Posing a question to your audience, besides involving them, wakes them up to what is being said. This works as fuel for a smooth transition to your next thought.

◆ Joke, Story, Anecdote or Quotation

Any of these can be used to first focus audience attention and thereafter connect with your point. It is an easy method but the choice of your narrative must be linked with the idea you intend presenting.

◆ Repetition

This involves wrapping up what you have just said and then merging it with the next idea. It helps build strong ties between different ideas. In a session on 'Inter-Personal Relationships' for housewives, for example, I said: 'We just discussed how you are responsible for creating a harmonious atmosphere at home. Now let's talk about what you could expect other family members to do . . .'.

◆ Specifying the Number of Points

If it is a short presentation you may like to, in the very beginning, specify that you have drafted your talk around three or four points. When I was delivering a fifteen minute talk on Positive Health to a group of women I decided to break up the topic into four parts. These were Physical, Mental, Emotional and Spiritual Health. When I was through with the physical aspects of one's health, I moved on to the next aspect and so on.

◆ Pauses

A brief break in your verbal delivery also indicates transition. A pause helps in gathering attention for what is about to be said. The pause should not be long, however, as that creates boredom and disinterest. Transition helps in creating harmony in the same way as shifting from one fret on to another in a musical instrument does.

8

THE FINAL ACT

E ven after thorough preparation, where considerable effort has gone into planning and rehearsing a presentation, many people are still concerned that something might go wrong on the final day! Sometimes the fear is that the speaker might forget what he intends saying, while at other times it is the uncertainty of the audience response which is a source of worry. You can master the skills of delivering effective speeches by working on these skills systematically over time.

Although we communicate mostly through words, it is surprising how little they contribute to the overall message. Research carried out to indicate the average percentage contribution of various components to the total communication process showed that we typically rely on the verbal, vocal and visual parts of communication to the extent shown:

- 7 per cent verbal (words, content, material, language used)

- 38 per cent vocal (voice, confidence in the voice, pace, modulation and enthusiasm)
- 55 per cent visual (facial expressions, gestures, posture, eye contact)

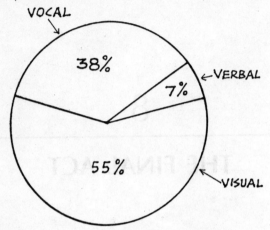

One has to learn, therefore, to be aware of not just what one is saying but also **how** one is saying it.

Query

I work hard at preparing my presentations. In fact, I write down my speech word for word. I then learn it by rote and deliver it as best I can. After all this effort, I still feel that the audience does not respond positively. They seem to be bored and disinterested. Where could the problem lie?

Response

Your problem seems to be that you are memorizing your speech! Once you do this you are bound to sound like a parrot.

A tip for a good presentation is to be natural and spontaneous. In effect, just be yourself. The words 'confidence' and 'fidelity' are both derived from the Latin root *fide* meaning truthfulness. It helps immensely to be true to oneself and not contrived.

You would, furthermore, need to develop a healthy rapport with the participants in the course of your presentation. Establishing eye contact with the entire group and making them feel respected is a good way to begin. Your level of enthusiasm and energy should be high as you can't expect a dynamic interaction when you yourself lack the needed drive or positive energy. Just rattling off a memorized speech will make for a bland presentation devoid of any real impact.

Stating facts, figures and data is crucial to many presentations. However, just harping on data, without any emotional involvement on your part, could make your presentation lacklustre.

Query

I know that maintaining eye contact is necessary for building a rapport with the audience but isn't it very difficult and often nerve-racking to look into people's eyes? What if it makes me forget what I have to say next?

Response

The first link you create while interacting with anyone is with the eyes. Imagine trying to communicate with your back towards somebody! Would you be able to reach out to him? Obviously not! Facing people in the audience gives you the opportunity to involve them in your speech. Believe it or not, considerable anxiety and tension is caused by looking away from the audience. When you cannot see them or gauge their reactions, you tend to imagine the worst and start feeling uncomfortable. Healthy eye contact (not staring) will put you at ease. Looking at the ceiling, hiding behind the whiteboard or the lectern, or peering out at the group are all detrimental to your role as speaker. Eye contact is akin to spelling out non-verbally: 'I wish to make contact with you'. If you find eye contact difficult it is probably because you've been unnecessarily avoiding it. Let your eyes roam freely over the audience. It will not be as nerve-racking as you think. Imagine models on the ramp, displaying outrageous outfits, who have scores of eyes peering at them!

And, if you fear that you will forget what you have to say by looking at your audience, make index cards which will remind you of your key thoughts.

Query

How can a speaker gauge audience reaction? Are there cues one can watch out for?

Response

Being sensitive to the audience's body movements will give you a fair idea of what they might be feeling or experiencing. The expressions on the face, the focus of the eyes etc. provide a further insight into what the audience might have on their minds. Some audience cues have precise meanings. For example:

• Looking away from the speaker	Shows distraction and disinterest.
• Crossing of arms or legs	A defensive posture indicating disagreement with the speaker.
• Shaking of the head	Depending on how this occurs, could indicate disagreement, disapproval or agreement.
• Leaning forward	Signals interest and eagerness or could also mean that the person is unable to hear you.
• Checking watch frequently	Indicates boredom. Also, the person looking at his watch may be late for another appointment.

Though these indicators might seem fairly obvious, one should learn to recognize them and be ready to respond to the feelings they reflect. It will help in keeping your audience interested. You need to be flexible and ready to adapt to the expectations of your audience. You may sometimes have to change the way you are expressing yourself if you sense audience boredom.

Query

One's quality of voice largely determines whether one is able to hold the audience's attention or not. What should be considered to improve the vocal factor of the presentation?

Response

Once you arrive to deliver a presentation, the audience sizes you up on the basis of your overall appearance and the way you carry yourself. Thereafter, the moment you start speaking, people either 'tune out' or develop a positive rapport and start 'resonating' with you. Your voice may exude confidence or represent the lack of it. There are three main factors that need attention as far as the vocal factor is concerned. These are:

◆ Volume

You could be speaking too loudly or softly. Good speakers need to be aware of this. During an actual presentation, you could even ask the audience whether they can hear you at the back of the room. Telling the audience that you are not able to speak out loud or that you are generally soft spoken is merely a case of stating a self-propagated myth! We can all raise our voices. Remember the time when you were last angry and how loud you were?

If you speak loudly under normal circumstances, you may need to get your hearing checked since it can indicate a slight hearing loss. Alternatively, it could be a habit. Consciously trying to reduce your volume would be helpful.

◆ Pace (Rate)

Our average conscious rate of speech is about 125 words per minute (w.p.m). When we are anxious the rate usually increases. An increased rate of speech is not really a problem if your articulation is fine. However, if you are making a technical presentation or one in which the audience wants to take notes you need to watch your pace. Sometimes one tends to gobble up the last few words of a sentence. You must try and speak every word completely and audibly. Pausing after explaining a concept is not a bad idea at all. Pauses help people absorb what they have heard and thereby understand better what you are saying. Don't be afraid to offer a few short periods of silence during your presentation. They only add value to what you have said.

While guarding against a fast pace, you need to be equally careful about a slow rate of speech which is, typically, less than 100 w.p.m. Speaking at this rate would distract your audience very easily and you would be unable to sustain their attention. Your pace could be slow because you have not prepared and are, therefore, thinking and speaking on the spot. The other problem could be poor control over the language. Searching for the right word, for example, could stall you.

◆ Tone/Modulation

A monotonous voice results from a speaker's anxiety. As the speaker becomes increasingly nervous, the muscles in his/her chest and throat become less flexible and the flow of air into the lungs is restricted. When this happens, the voice loses its natural intonation and variation. To bring back the variety of tone you need to relax in order to release the tension.

Learn to loosen your muscles and breathe normally before a speech, even if you are a little nervous. This skill can be developed and practised. Emphasizing particular ideas or words then becomes correspondingly easier. This, in turn, will help focus the attention of the audience. The ability to utilize the full range of your vocal 'spectrum' is one of the keys to your success as a presenter.

The quality of your voice is also linked to your attitude. While making your presentation, if you try and maintain a positive, sincere and helpful approach it will always show up in your vocal attributes. When you feel good, you will sound good.

Query

Once in a while, when I don't enjoy listening to a speaker, I realise the problem may be voice-related. What are the specific pitfalls in this area that one should guard against?

Response

Enquiries concerning the vocal attributes of a good speaker have resulted in responses such as sweet, melodious, warm, pleasant, etc. Of course, we would all like our voices to possess such qualities but we aren't all as gifted. A few speech problems that should be guarded against are:

◆ Straining Your Voice Box

You may have developed a speaking pattern whereby you over use your vocal cords. Your listeners want to hear you speak, not shout. If your muscles have become taut while speaking and you are under undue and unnecessary stress, try and loosen up. Relaxing will help you and your voice.

◆ Not Throwing Your Voice

I have encountered many speakers who are constantly asked to repeat what they have said as they haven't been heard. They seem to be playing the game of 'whispering words'! If you are one of them, learn to speak from your belly and not just your throat. 'Throwing' or 'projecting' your voice is necessary. Some degree of the right attitude is also a must. Being enthused enough to address a group reflects your energy, vitality and dynamism. Your voice will automatically support you in communicating these positive feelings.

◆ Nasal Speech

I think it is more out of habit that some people speak through their noses. It proves to be a big distraction, besides sounding unpleasant. It is quite simple to shift your focus from the nose to the mouth. Constant practice will help in this regard.

◆ Dry and Hoarse Throat

I have found myself confronted with this condition often. During long workshops the throat, with over-use and strain, tends to become dry and tired sometimes resulting in a cough. My remedy is to carry lozenges and keep a jar of water always close by. A check-up by your doctor might be necessary if you suffer from this condition frequently. If there is nothing wrong medically, then you are just not using your breath adequately to support your voice. What results is a croaky voice which irritates you as well as your audience.

Query

When people talk of body language, what are they actually talking about?

Response

Quite a substantial contribution to your message is made by the things that you don't actually say: the way you choose to stand, the gestures you use, whether you look happy or sad and a whole array of non-verbal cues besides. All these non-verbal signals are referred to as 'body language'. Being sensitive and aware of your body language is essential to presenting a forceful and effective verbal message. If the body language and the spoken communication are not congruent, the audience actually tends to believe the non-verbal message! In Chapter 2, the various aspects of body language have been discussed in detail.

CONFIDENT   AGGRESSIVE   SUBMISSIVE

Query

Even after having prepared my presentation and practised my speech thoroughly, I still feel nervous and fearful when I find myself facing the audience. Is it something I have to learn to bear or can I do something about it?

Response

Franklin Roosevelt once said that the only thing we need fear is fear itself! Anxiety is a very natural emotion arising whenever stress occurs. The thought of making a presentation does induce stress, causing symptoms such as stomach churning, sweaty palms, jelly-like legs, rapid breathing and a pounding heart! The first step you can take to combat nervousness is to accept these symptoms as natural. Now let us consider other ways and means of dealing with these feelings.

◆ Prepare Thoroughly

Being well-prepared reduces nervousness to a large degree.

Knowing what you have to say and when you plan to say it will help ease your nerves. When your thoughts are well structured and you have confidence cards that serve as a memory aid, you are bound to feel confident. These index or confidence cards contain a list of the key ideas of your presentation in sequential order. Index cards can be made of any thick paper and should measure approximately 5 in. × 3 in.

◆ Visualize Success

Imagining doing a great job instead of thinking about the worst truly works. Speakers who fail to deliver good presentations first fail in their own minds since their thoughts are self-defeating. Try and visualize success—the power this unleashes is immense. You should always make your thoughts work for you rather than against your goals.

◆ Practice, Practice and Practice

Practice makes a good presentation perfect! Adequate confidence is gained when a presentation is rehearsed thoroughly prior to the final day. You may otherwise find yourself bungling your way through the presentation.

◆ Breathe Deeply

Whenever you are worked up, your muscles tighten and your breathing becomes shallow. Once that happens, you cannot throw your voice across. This further adds to the stress. To avoid this vicious cycle, start by taking a few deep breaths. You will feel the difference immediately. Breathing and relaxation are interconnected. The better and easier you breathe, the more relaxed you will feel.

◆ Focus on Relaxing and Releasing Tension

Instead of thinking about the tension you feel, focus on relaxing. Speak to yourself and affirm your well-being with some positive 'self-talk' such as: 'I am relaxed', 'I am incharge', 'I will make a great presentation', and so on. This also helps release pent-up tension just prior to going on stage. A simple way to do this is to first tighten your muscles and then relax them. You can start from your toes and move gradually upwards to your calf muscles, thighs, stomach, hands and neck. This method works well in reducing accumulated negative energy.

◆ Maintain Eye Contact

Maintaining healthy eye contact with your audience will help you relax. You will realize, when you make eye contact, that your audience is as human as you are. A wonderful connection is thus created which helps immensely.

◆ Anticipate Questions

Your anxiety could arise from the thought that the audience is bound to ask questions to which you have no answers! While preparing, take care to plan for questions that you might be asked. There could still be the odd member of audience who might question you relentlessly, keen to pull you up and ensure you lose your confidence. A good speaker has to learn how to handle such difficult or aggressive participants.

◆ Stop Worrying About Yourself

If you start worrying about the feelings you are experiencing before the presentation, you will only make matters worse. Instead, look 'outward' and try to forget your own nervous symptoms. You are the only one who knows about your thumping heart and the cold sweat in your palms! Others cannot even remotely sense that you are experiencing these feelings, especially if you pay no heed to them yourself. So, just move away from yourself and your feelings and start connecting with the audience.

◆ Movement

Moving around physically before your presentation either in a corridor, a wash room, or anywhere quiet and private will help you relax. Being rooted to a spot can enhance your feelings of nervousness. So make yourself comfortable by pacing up and down the hallway for a few minutes before your presentation is due!

✦ Believe in the Warmth of the Audience

Believe that your audience is friendly, which it usually is. It is better to treat your listeners as your allies rather than perceive them as your competitors. This belief will bring you closer to them and put you at ease.

If you practise these techniques, there will no longer be any need to face that gnawing nervousness each time you take the stage.

9

VISUALS FOR IMPACT

Some of the world's best speakers are men and women who speak from their hearts without the use of props, audio-visual aids or even a lectern! In fact, some of the world's greatest speakers have been its leaders and philosophers such as, Gautama Buddha, Prophet Mohammed, Jesus Christ, Guru Gobind Singh, Osho Rajneesh, Joan of Arc and Martin Luther King. None of them ever used audio-visual aids. Their personal magnetism was so intense that they had no need for such external aids. Moreover, they were absolutely clear about what they had to say and did so with passion and conviction.

In today's world of television and radio advertisements and a whole host of other distractions and noise, a good presenter has to somehow ensure that his or her presentation stands out and is heard. Simultaneously, the message has to be understood too. Under such circumstances, the use of audio-visuals is not just recommended, but is desirable as well.

Any speaker can benefit from the use of audio-visuals. These are especially helpful when you want to:

- Focus the attention of the audience on something.
- Reinforce your spoken message.
- Stimulate additional interest.
- Show a diagram or a table with information that is otherwise difficult to visualize.

Visual aids are, however, just a means to an end. Many speakers fall into the trap of substituting what they have to say by audio-visuals. A selection of the ideas you wish to communicate should form the core of your presentation; one can then develop visuals to express these ideas with more efficacy.

Don't ever use visual aids to do any of these:

- Impress your audience with detailed graphs and tables.
- Avoid interaction with your audience.
- Present simple ideas that can be better expressed verbally.

Visuals must complement your presentation, not take over your role as a speaker. Remember, you are your best audio-visual!

Query

Even when one dares use audio-visual aids, many a time there are last-minute hitches. Can some quick checks help to avoid this?

Response

You must, as an effective presenter, plan and prepare your audio-visuals in advance. Besides, the effectiveness of your audio-visuals will depend largely on whether you can use them the way you intend. A few cues to avoid last-minute hitches are:

- You must set up and arrange all the equipment and infrastructure needed well before the audience arrives. It is important that you are comfortable with the controls of the computer, the slide projector, the OHP or any other device you may be using.

- For the overhead and slide projectors, check that the screen is properly positioned and unaffected by bright natural light.

- For films and slides, check which switches you would need and whether the picture fits the screen.

- Check that your visuals are visible from every seat. Nobody should feel left out.

- Avoid depending on rented equipment which will arrive only a few minutes before you are due to start.

Query

How can one make the best use of visual presentation material?

Response

To make your visuals work for you, just remember the following:

- Use your visuals sparingly. One of the biggest problems in technical presentations is the use of too many visuals. A useful rule to remember is: use a visual not more than every three or four minutes of presentation time.

- Use pictorial visuals such as graphs, pictures, flowcharts. All these help create a lasting impression on the mind of the listener and have more impact than plain text.

- One idea per visual is far better than squeezing in everything you want to say onto a single slide.

- Make your text and numbers legible. A minimum font size of 20 points is recommended for a room set-up. It can be very frustrating for the audience if they can't read what has been written on the visual. They must be able to see your visual without strain even from the last row.

- Use colours in visuals to make them more interesting. However, be careful not to use more than three or four colours per visual. The colours used must contrast with each other for better effect.

- Choose graphs instead of tables. A graphical representation explains ideas better and faster than information in a tabular form.

- Keep away from 'miscellaneous' visuals. If something can be stated verbally why use a visual at all?

- Show a visual which is relevant to what you are talking about. If there is something particular on the screen but you are speaking of something else, your audience is bound to be distracted and confused. Your visuals must be in line with what you are saying at any given moment. Leaving a written word on a white/blackboard while you have moved away from that topic is undesirable. If another speaker has left visible signs on a whiteboard or flipchart, remove these first and then proceed.

Query

What are the common presentation tools I can choose from?

Response

Any device that helps you achieve your presentation objective can be termed an effective tool. Common ones are:

- Slides—Either foils for an overhead projector or 36 mm transparencies that require a slide projector.
- 8 mm/16 mm films and videotapes.
- LCD and DLP projectors.
- Laptops.
- Multimedia.
- Charts, large photographic displays or exhibits such as working-models and prototypes.
- Black- or Whiteboards.
- Flipcharts.
- Handouts.
- Props (such as those used by magicians).
- Pantomime (done by the presenter or trained actors).

Each one of the above has its own set of advantages and disadvantages. You must consider what would suit your communication needs and the presentation environment, and thereafter make your selection. Keep in mind, however, that you must not get carried away with the special effects.

Query

As there are so many aids one can choose from, how do I decide what to use?

Response

Let us analyze the major advantages and disadvantages of these aids.

Sildes

You could select between the overhead slide or the 36 mm slide.

◆ Overhead Slides

Advantages
- Can be pre-prepared.

- Can be used for large groups and with normal lighting.
- Enable you to speak facing the audience while your visual is showing.
- Enable you to reveal your material gradually, point by point, through the use of 'overlay' (putting one slide over another), or even by building on an existing transparency.
- Can be produced easily and inexpensively.
- Can be made in colour.

Disadvantages
- Require large storage space and are difficult to keep clean.
- Could cause you to go out of sequence during your presentation if the number of slides used is high.
- Difficult to show three-dimensional pictures or anything as complex.
- Difficult to keep the image square when being used for large audiences.

◆ Slide Projector

Advantages
- Reproduction is sharp and excellent in colour.
- Easy to store and update.
- Can be remote-controlled by the speaker.
- 36 mm cameras are easy to use and are portable.
- Can be synchronized with sound.
- Multi image capabilities allow simultaneous comparison.

Disadvantages
- Can be easily projected out of sequence, upside down or backwards.
- Room needs to be partially darkened. This can sometimes alienate the audience.
- Slides get damaged over time.
- Speaker can be obscured and sometimes forgotten. The audience may become too involved with the visuals.
- Projector can malfunction.
- Preparation time needed is greater.
- Note-taking is difficult.

Flipchart

Advantages
- Can be pre-prepared and used directly in the presentation.
- Can refer back to a particular page/sheet as there is a written record.
- Very inexpensive and no special skills are needed to produce or use it.
- Can be made colourful by the simple use of colour marker pens.

Disadvantages
- Limited to small audiences.
- Difficult to explain and look at the audience at the same time.
- Cannot show or draw complex graphics during the presentation.
- Difficult to carry the easel which holds the flipchart.
- Does not look as professional as slides.

Computer-based Presentations

Advantages
- Very professional and creates tremendous interest.
- Full-colour multimedia presentations can be created.
- Last-minute changes are possible.
- Data can be presented in real time.
- Transmission to remote locations is possible.
- Production costs are low.

Disadvantages
- Equipment is expensive.
- Computer handling and usage skills are needed.
- Presentation can replace the presenter.
- A partially darkened room is required.
- Every venue is not equipped with the requisite infrastructure.
- The time required for setting up such a presentation is high.

Motion Pictures

Advantages
- Gains instant attention and involves the audience completely.
- Colourful and dynamic.
- Different angles and dimensions can be focussed on making perception clear.

Disadvantages
- Room has to be completely darkened causing the link between the presenter and the audience to snap.
- Transition from the film show back to reality, i.e. the speaker, might be difficult.
- Expensive to produce.
- Selecting an appropriate film and then hiring the venue/equipment can be cumbersome and time consuming.

Videotape

Advantages
- Tape is reusable.
- Simple to operate.
- Full motion capabilities.
- Colour possibility.
- Easy back and forth movement of the tape.

Disadvantages
- Recording equipment is expensive.
- Some formats are incompatible on the playback equipment.
- Playback equipment is costly and the rental can be high.
- Difficult to use in large groups.

Query

There is a lot being said about the use of newer technologies like computers in making presentations. What really goes into it?

Response

The growth of information technology has meant growth in the field of presentations as well. People now rely extensively on computers for making presentations. You can merge pictures and sound on your computer and then project it directly from the computer onto a screen. To do this you need to use both the hardware and the software of the computer. Aspects of the former that you may need for a presentation include:

◆ Printer

You can use a colour printer to print directly onto an acetate.

◆ CD-Rom Players

There is abundant information available on Compact Discs. They can store video and audio clips and other information that can be handy for your presentation.

◆ Scanner

This allows you to take a picture or any other text and digitize it. You can then use it in whatever way you wish.

◆ Monitor

Their quality has been improving by the day to keep pace with the upgradation of computers.

◆ Projection Devices

A number of devices are available in the market that allow the computer screen to be projected onto a larger screen.

There are three main types of software used in the production of the presentation. These are:

◆ Word Processing Software

These programmes can be used to prepare overhead transparencies or slides. You can vary the font size and present the basic data along with some visuals.

◆ Presentation Software

These programmes are a little more complex and require some training before they can be used. If you do make regular presentations with visuals then learning and using the presentation software will be worthwhile.

Most of these programmes have pre-designed templates which add a lot of value to a presentation. One can select diagrams, graphics and photographs and use them by changing their size and position. A combination of text and visuals is possible. You can make a few formats and then view them a couple of times to decide what you would prefer to use.

◆ Graphics Software

These allow the user to create different kinds of graphics including three dimensional ones. They are particularly useful for research and technical presentations.

Query

Are there any design aspects that need to be considered to make computer presentations look more professional?

Response

There is bound to be a difference between random placing of material on a visual and a systematic designing of its content. Planning the layout, the text and the graphics among other aspects makes a remarkable difference to the overall quality of the visual.

What you need to consider is:

◆ Layout

The choice is between landscape and portrait. The general rule followed is that visuals are made horizontally (landscape) as against vertically (portrait). One reason is that a horizontal image can be seen at one go. Also, more space is available when using such an image. Portrait visuals contain the danger of the bottom not being visible.

When a visual is shown, the eyes naturally land at the optical centre of the screen, a spot slightly above and to the left of the centre. Therefore all text should be arranged to read from left to right.

♦ Text

You will find some visuals more appealing than others. Obviously the presenter has incorporated certain methods in presenting the information which has succeeded in holding the attention of the audience. Some of these methods are:

Bullets. Use of bullets is a simple yet powerful technique to display various points of information. It also helps you remember the points of your presentation.

Builds. These help the viewers focus on one idea at a time. When you move to the next idea, the previous one can be shown in a smaller font or a lighter colour.

Desktop presentation software can create builds easily. You can even design a visual where each point is further elaborated by animation effects.

Less clutter. Visuals should be kept crisp and concise. The 6×6 rule is a good rule to follow, i.e., six words per sentence and not more than six sentences in a visual. It reduces clutter, to begin with. Moreover, in the time you are giving the viewer (about 10–15 seconds) per visual, you can't squeeze in much more.

Parallel construction. Points on the visual should follow a scheme of parallel construction. For example, if the first bullet point starts with a noun, make sure the subsequent ones follow the same pattern.

♦ Typography

The actual writing on the visual needs as much planning and selection as the other aspects.

The font size should be 20 points or above. Any less than this will be too small and will not show well. The headings can be made larger than the sub-headings and the main content.

Avoid writing everything in upper case. It proves more difficult to read than the combination of upper and lower case.

You have a choice of fonts available but some display better. Sans serif fonts such as 'Helvetica' work better than ones with detailed features such as 'Times'. Try to stick to the one or two fonts that you have selected. Changing fonts for each visual may not go down well with your audience.

Abbreviations and unfamiliar jargon should be kept to a minimum unless the audience is well acquainted with it.

◆ Graphics

A picture is definitely more powerful than simple text. You can use clip art or even scanned art to demonstrate and illustrate an idea Remember, whatever picture you decide to use must complement your presentation.

◆ Graphs and Diagrams

These help immensely in showing changes, highlighting comparisons and establishing links. You can use pie charts, bar graphs or line graphs.

Diagrams help the viewer understand ideas, concepts, plans, and sequences. Flowcharts, and organizational charts are two such examples.

◆ Templates

One feature of most computer-based presentations is the use of professionally designed templates. A template signifies a particular background including both the design and the scheme to be followed throughout the presentation.

Aspects of a template (colour, fonts, sizes) can be changed to suit your needs.

✦ Colour

Use colour to add colour to your presentation! Contrast helps. You can limit your use to two or three colours and use these well.

Studies have shown that we retain information in a variety of ways and in varying degrees. It has been established that we retain 10 per cent of what we read, 20 per cent of what we hear, 30 per cent of what we see and 50 per cent of what we see and hear. Other studies suggest that seeing teaches us more than 75 per cent of what we learn. No doubt the right audio-visuals will create the right impact on the audience. However, at the risk of being repetitive, the best audio-visual anytime, anywhere is YOU.

10

HANDLING QUESTIONS, OBJECTIONS AND DIFFICULT PARTICIPANTS

Even if your presentation is lucid and clearly meets the audience's expectations, it would be unwise to think that there will be no questions on what you have said. An effective presentation may not elicit *too many* questions but you must prepare for the likelihood of some being asked.

The way you answer and handle audience questions will determine the overall impact of your presentation. Many speakers do an excellent job of delivering their talk but ruin the whole presentation by answering questions shoddily! Apart from wanting further information and seeking genuine clarifications on doubts, your audience might ask questions for any of the following reasons:

- To gain attention (yes, there are people who love making a point largely to gain attention!).
- To display their knowledge and erudition (these people often fall into the first category!).
- To relieve their boredom.
- To lead the speaker onto another subject or away from the one being spoken about.
- To voice their concerns.

And, finally, in the rare but not unknown situation,

- To actually disrupt your speech.

Knowing and understanding *why* a person is asking a certain question will help you answer it with sensitivity. You are thereby in a better position to satisfy the questioner. The audience feels glad when a speaker answers a question with empathy. Try not to solicit questions during your presentation. Interruptions can disrupt the flow of your message and may prove detrimental to the efficacy of the presentation. I think taking up questions at the end of a presentation is a good idea. Apart from being more convenient and economical from the point of view of time, it is better that the audience know comprehensively all that you have in mind. After they have heard you completely, their question/s may be naturally answered during the course of your presentation. But if someone does have a genuine query that arises in the midst of your talk, don't leave the questioner unsatisfied. Clarify the questioner's doubts and proceed further. This shows your concern and your audience is bound to appreciate it.

Query

Are there any general guidelines to follow while answering questions from the audience?

Response

As with most other skills, the ability to handle questions also improves as we do more of it. You will learn to respond appropriately as you learn to survive the onslaught of audience questions. Yet a few guidelines, if kept in mind, will help. These are:

- Concentrate totally on the individual who has asked the question and look directly at him/her while the question is being asked. Do not fiddle with your material or look at anything else. In doing so you are not showing adequate interest or respect for your questioner which are essential prerequisites for handling questions effectively.

- Listen for the content *and* intent of the question. The facial expressions and body language of the questioner will indicate what and why the question is being posed. Even the tone of voice will signal whether the query or concern is genuine or not.

- After you have heard the question, repeat the question in your own words. This helps confirm that you have heard right what was being asked and also helps the rest of the audience hear the question clearly. Besides, paraphrasing the question also confirms that the ideas conveyed have been understood as intended.

- Ask for clarifications if the question is not clear.

- Answer the question clearly, specifically and briefly. There is no need for you to make another presentation in answer to a question!

- Verify that the listener is satisfied with your answer. If you feel that your answer has not fully reassured the questioner, you must be willing to share further evidence or data that will reinforce your message.

- Avoid getting into a one-to-one conversation with the person who has asked the question. After acknowledging the questioner, look out at the entire audience and answer them all. Of course, you can keep reassuring the questioner by looking at him once in a while.

- Break up a complex, *many-questions-rolled into-one* query into separate questions and answer them one by one, part by part.

- If you don't know the answer to a question, admit it. Beating about the bush never helps. An honest 'I don't know, but I will find out' is a far more open, assertive and respectful way to respond to the audience.

- Be factual and accurate. A quick answer, unsupported by specific evidence, is not appreciated. Avoid using phrases like 'They say . . .' or 'A recent report highlighted . . .'. Be specific and state accurate facts.

- Solicit questions from all within the audience—those in the front, at the back, the sides, or in the aisles. Don't just focus on one area or individual. Everybody wants to be involved and that needs to be encouraged.

Query

Are there some definitive 'dont's' advocated while responding to queries?

Response

There are definitely some things to avoid while answering questions. These are:

- Avoid using phrases such as, 'That is a good question' or 'That is a silly query'. Take the questions as they come and answer them without being judgmental.

- Don't argue with the audience. You are not competing with them.

- Don't allow one person to keep on asking the questions. In a friendly but assertive way make him aware that others have doubts too.

- Don't stand with your hands on your hips or frown unnecessarily while you are responding to questions. You must watch your body language and ensure it is friendly rather than threatening. Some speakers do tend to feel 'threatened' if they perceive their presentation under 'attack'.

- Don't wag your finger at the questioner. You are not preaching but presenting an idea.

- Don't use phrases such as 'Anyone will know the answer to that one . . . ' or 'Well, obviously . . . '. These phrases may insult and embarrass the questioner and the audience.

    If you keep these points in mind, you can't go wrong!

Query

Many a time I have encountered difficult people in the audience. These are people who either don't want to listen patiently or want to create an impression by dominating the discussion. At times, however, I come across totally reticent people in the audience. I am confused about how I should deal with a varied audience?

Response

Those listening to your presentation will come in all hues. This holds true in any speaking situation. It will be helpful if you can identify the kind of participants you are likely to be dealing with and then contemplate handling them accordingly. Problem people you would come across generally fall into the following broad categories:

◆ The Aggressor

This person always thinks he is right. You may be able to win him over with facts and logic. If that fails, then it is best to ignore this person. You must keep your cool. Agreeing with some of his ideas, if they are constructive, may be a good strategy. He will feel good, as a result, and that would make life easier.

◆ The Intelligent Talker

This member of the audience is sharp and he wants that to be known. He might end up doing a lot of extra talking. This will cause the audience to feel left out besides causing envy and anger. To deal with him you will have to assert yourself and

make sure you distribute audience airtime evenly. Once again, it helps to use his intelligence for the benefit of the group and your presentation.

◆ The Sceptical One

This individual is averse to all new ideas. To deal with him you will need to address his doubts with compassion and understanding. Assure him of the benefits that will accrue if he chooses to open up and consider new ideas. A good suggestion from such a person should not be ignored. When you accept his point of view chances are that he will be more willing to accept yours.

◆ The Shy Kind

This person is timid and retiring. You can help him 'open up' by granting him importance. You could ask him a direct question which you are sure he will be able to answer. Acknowledging his response will encourage him and prompt him to participate further.

Since the audience at any presentation may include individuals who belong to all or some of the above categories, you need to be adept at handling people who exhibit such varied behavioural patterns. With regular and frequent interactions, you will gain in experience about the realm of human behaviour and will accordingly learn to modify your own style to create synergy and harmony between yourself and your audience.

11

SPECIAL SPEECHES

There are a number of occasions when one is called upon to make a presentation *about another presentation*! This is not a rare occurrence at all, as many of you would agree. In many formal situations where presentations are made, someone else has to serve as the 'vehicle' between the audience and the main speaker.

There is, however, a distinctive difference between being a presenter yourself and presenting some information connected with someone else's speech. Preparing and making a presentation on your own is a different 'cup of tea' altogether as compared to making a 'special occasion' speech. Special occasion speeches could include: introducing a speaker or the subject of a speaker's speech, proposing a vote of thanks, or making a farewell speech in honour of an employee who is leaving your firm. While the basics of good communication remain the same, making any of these special, event-oriented speeches requires you to be especially sensitive about:

- The speaker.
- The subject.
- The audience.
- The event-organizer.
- Other event details.

An occasion speech can be made at either the beginning or the close of an event. Often such speeches are called for at the start *and* at the end of the event. This would, of course, depend on the format of the function or event and how the organizers wish to showcase the main component of the function.

Occasion speeches are made to celebrate, entertain or just create the right atmosphere for an event. Planning and preparation are as important for an event speech as for a presentation. Being caught on the wrong foot or being taken by surprise is something all speakers can do without. So be ready in the event that you may have to make a special speech.

Query

Speakers making presentations are often introduced formally. Is this necessary?

Response

It is. Introducing a speaker helps you create for her a conducive ambience. It ensures the audience pays complete and respectful attention to the speaker. A formal introduction is equivalent to building a bridge between the audience and the presenter.

Introducing a speaker is one of the main 'starting-off activities' in the context of an event. Never take this assignment in a non-serious, unprofessional way. If you are ever chosen for this task, try and do your utmost to ensure the audience is left eagerly looking forward to the main event.

Query

Are there any ground rules and guidelines to follow while introducing a speaker?

Response

You may have found introductions either too long, not properly delivered or, for some other reason, not able to elicit the right kind of response from the audience. Therefore, it is necessary to learn the right way of introducing a speaker.

- Keep the speech brief. Three minutes or less is ideal.
- Understand your audience and their needs. You should be able to portray the speaker in a way that is relevant to the audience.
- Don't add unnecessary superlatives while describing your speaker. His resume or bio-data should prove a good guide. You should go by what is mentioned in it. Exaggerating never helps. On the other hand, it only creates added pressure on the speaker to perform.
- Avoid mentioning anything that is irrelevant to the subject or the audience. Sharing anything that you might know about the speaker on a personal level is never a good idea.
- Pronounce the speaker's name correctly and say it loud enough for others to hear. Ask the speaker beforehand how he wants his name pronounced if you are unsure about it.
- Introduce the speaker in a warm, friendly and cordial manner. What you feel about the speaker is bound to reflect on your countenance. Therefore, you need to be enthused about the speaker, the topic and his presence. This message will then communicate itself to the audience.
- Even if you know something about the topic, don't be tempted into speaking on it. This is not your job.

Query

Sometimes invited speakers hand over a couple of pages stating their achievements. If I have to introduce such a speaker, what do I do with so much information? How do I keep it short?

Response

It is prudent to ask the speaker for his bio-data well in advance. This gives you time to assess what you should include. Keeping the audience profile in mind will help in the screening process. Use your judgement to further assist you in deciding what the speaker would like to hear about himself. A detailed bio-data will call for the extensive use of your editing skills. But make sure while deleting information that you do not edit out anything important.

Query

Even after minor events, one finds a 'vote of thanks' (VOT) being delivered. It seems like a waste of time. Why do we need this formality?

Response

When somebody visits you or you visit somebody, do you need to think twice before saying 'thanks'? I am sure not. A vote of thanks is a similar expression of gratitude. It is made on behalf of the audience and is aimed at conveying appreciation for the speaker's efforts. In the way that a good dessert adds value to a meal, a proper VOT does the same to a presentation. It also leaves the speaker with a good feeling about the group he has just addressed. If you are proposing a vote of thanks for a big function or event, do take note of all the people and agencies who have contributed towards making the event successful. This list should include your sponsors, the organizers and the back-stage team. Even those who provide the infrastructure and resources like the sound/light systems and the catering deserve a mention. And finally, you should say a word or two about the people who have patiently heard out the speaker. In simple words, the vote of thanks helps you communicate your appreciation for all those who have had a role to play in the making of the event.

Query

How can a vote of thanks be delivered effectively?

Response

All communication can be effective provided you plan and prepare well. The various ideas that need to be kept in mind to deliver an effective vote of thanks are:

- Remember the mnemonic KISS: Keep It Short and Simple.
- Don't get carried away with your speech. The main event is over and your job is to wind up.
- You can highlight the main ideas of the presentation if your speech allows it. You could also emphasize the action points that the audience need to undertake.
- When you say 'thank you' it should be heartfelt. This is a prerequisite for a good vote of thanks. An insincere **VOT** is demeaning for all concerned.
- This is not the time to ask further questions and trigger a discussion. Queries and clarifications should have been addressed during or immediately after the main presentation itself.
- When you are satisfied that you have said all you had set out to, you should stop. When the drill bit strikes water, the drill has to stop.

Query

Some of our team members had been awarded by the company for their performance and we were acknowledging this with a celebration in the department. One of our senior colleagues was asked to speak. He went 'off-track', giving a full-fledged speech. How can we avoid such situations?

Response

Remember that a celebration is a celebration, irrespective of where it is being held. It is a time for togetherness and an occasion for the office staff to bond. A few pointers in this direction are:

- Don't make it a technical presentation. Work-related information should be avoided.

- Try to help make the atmosphere as relaxed as possible.

- Instead of reiterating the 'I' in your speech, use the '**We**' more frequently.

- Keep your presentation brief. Your speech is more likely a ritual, so don't make it tedious.

- You should be aware of the objective of the celebration. This will help you structure the content of your talk.

- If an individual or individuals in office are the centre of attraction, let them remain so. Find out more about them from colleagues and weave your communication around that information. Focus on the personal rather than the professional.

- Acknowledge the person and her work adequately.

- You could search for additional information or a newspaper/magazine article in connection with the person being spoken about. This will demonstrate the effort and care that you have taken for the event.

- Avoid mentioning anything that could embarrass the awardees.

- If you have organized for a gift or any other form of recognition (which you should), take care that it has been brought to the venue.

- Don't exaggerate or over-dramatize events. Stick to factual information.

- Your choice of words should be appropriate. For example instead of saying 'These awards could have been received much earlier if enough effort had been put in', you could say 'These awards are well deserved and mean much to all of us here'.

Query

I often find myself taken by surprise when I am invited, without any prior indication, to speak at some forum. How do I tackle these impromptu speech opportunities with ease?

Response

Whenever you find yourself in such a situation, the first prerequisite is to remain calm. Do not panic. If you have been asked to speak or answer some query, it obviously indicates that people are reposing their faith in your skill and experience. Try not to let them down. Gear up, bolster your confidence, take a few deep breaths and start. A few additional steps you could take, which might prove helpful, are:

◆ Think Fast

The capacity to think swiftly is a big boon. You could start by clarifying the purpose of the speech, thinking of material related to your topic, and trying to organize the content in a specific pattern. You could use the past, present and future structure or a categorical organization—both of which have been described in Chapter 7.

◆ Then Deliver

Before you actually get to the main body of your speech, take some time to make introductory remarks. This will help you relax and also give you some breathing space. You could start by saying, for example, 'I'm pleased to be with you and want to inform you about . . .'

Then, say something about the focus of your speech. Finally, a strong crescendo-like movement to conclude will leave a lasting impact.

Use examples and analogies to support your ideas. If you are a regular speaker or find yourself often making impromptu speeches, then do keep yourself prepared with short, crispy anecdotes, examples and quotations. Be prepared, yet be spontaneous enough to sound natural. As George Bernard Shaw once said: 'I'm the most spontaneous speaker in the world, because every word, every gesture and every retort has been carefully rehearsed'.

Part Three

PRESENTATIONS MADE BY DIFFERENT PROFESSIONALS

12

SALES PRESENTATIONS

Being in sales necessitates making frequent presentations. With time, sales personnel generally master this skill but it is helpful to be aware of the ingredients that make for outstanding sales presentations. This chapter will tell you what you would need to do to make your presentation powerful.

Typically, sales presentations are made to different groups of people. You could either be addressing a prospective client or the territory development manager. You might even have to make a presentation to a potential collaborator. Whoever the audience, sales presentations have one overriding objective: namely, to **convince** the listener. The listener could either be the buyer of your products, services or ideas, or the distributor of your goods. At the end of the presentation the audience must believe in and accept what you are offering.

SALES PRESENTATIONS

The format of a sales presentation must follow the broad sequence indicated below:

- Outlining the need for the 'offering'.
- Proving the offering has the potential to satisfy the listener's needs or solve a vexing problem of his.
- Demonstrating the listener can afford to purchase the offering on the terms indicated.

As with all good speakers, a sales professional has to spend time planning and preparing her presentation for it to have the desired impact.

Preparation

While planning a presentation, keep the prospects of the sale in mind. The presentation can then be tailor-made.

A sales person should also understand the difference between the features of a product and its benefits to the user. For example, you could be selling calculators, but the focus of your presentation will have to be on the speed and accuracy of calculation and the improvement it brings to office efficiency.

Similarly, you could be propagating ideas for a superior form of skill development, but what you will need to highlight for the benefit of the listener will be career success or personal development. Charles Revson of Revlon cosmetics once said '*in the factory we manufacture cosmetics, but to our customers we sell hope*'. This lucidly sums up how a presenter has to offer his wares!

While preparing for a presentation you will have to gather relevant up-to-date information about the company you represent including current prices and, if applicable, the kind of discounts/schemes being offered on products.

One of the important parameters of a good sales presentation is the logical structuring of the material. It should also be easy to understand. Putting yourself in the customer's shoes and thinking from his perspective will help you weave a proper sequence of ideas. If there has been a prior understanding or commitment made to the client, review the contents of such a commitment carefully before the presentation and be ready with any related information that the client might seek.

Planning for a sales presentation would also require you to decide on the appropriate medium for use. Pictures always speak better than words. You also have to decide on the use of appropriate audio-visuals and accordingly, acquire the necessary equipment and infrastructue (cf. Chapter 9, 'Visuals for Impact').

You cannot close a sale without a few objections being raised by the prospective buyer. This is one consideration that separates sales presentations from other presentations. Being well-prepared with the right responses to likely objections is part of the preparation that you, as an effective sales person, will have to rigorously undergo.

It will be of great help if you can collect testimonials from other satisfied customers as proof of the superior service that your company offers. Carrying such testimonials along and using them in your presentation will increase your credibility.

Delivery and Personal Style

All sales persons have unique presentation styles. With time, of course, you will realize that there are some distinctive things you will need to bear in mind if you wish to make an effective presentation. Some pointers in this direction:

◆ 1. Open with Impact

- The first few minutes that you spend with your clients could either make or undo the sale.
- A few successful openers are:
  - Rhetorical questions such as, '*Do you know how our product meets your needs? Our team has looked into this and I plan today to present findings based on our extensive research*'.
  - A successful sales story.
  - A unique bonus or discount that your company is offering.
  - The 'curiosity approach': where you sell an idea that tickles the sense of the client. For example, '*What would you say if I were to save your company five million rupees a year?*'
  - A shocking statement which helps gain the immediate attention and interest of the client. For example, '*Are you aware that your expensive process computers can badly malfunction if penetrated by fine dust?*' This could be the sales pitch of a sales person selling air purifiers to a client whose use of process computers is high.

◆ 2. Keep it Short and Simple

Many sales persons think that being verbose helps. On the contrary. Being able to convey the most important aspects of your offer in the least amount of time is important.

Mark Twain had once gone to listen to a presentation where the objective of the organizers was to collect money for charity. When the speaker started, Mr. Twain mentally decided to donate $ 100. But then the speaker went on and on, and he finally gave only $ 1. Mark Twain, handing him the dollar, said

'*You have just talked yourself out of $ 99*'. Good presenters are sensitive enough to know when to stop.

◆ 3. Avoid the Use of Jargon and Complex Technical Terms

Remind yourself that the use of simple terms is better and sells more goods. Sales people often share with their clients technical and commercial details of the product or service which has nothing to do with the benefits being offered them. Harping on the benefits, on the other hand, helps the customer make a quick decision.

◆ 4. Create a Relaxed Selling Ambience

Being uptight while communicating with the client can create a stressful atmosphere. This never helps in building a relationship with the client. A tense, nervous sales person can also put the customer on edge. On the other hand, keeping communication channels open by asking appropriate questions and listening with empathy go a long way in involving and collaborating with the audience.

◆ 5. Hone Your Communication Ability

Remember, there is a difference between telling and selling. And this difference is based essentially on the tone of voice used and the extent of vocal variety. You need to work on your voice and the parameters that define it. You should sound pleasant and natural, speak at the right volume and with clarity, and of course manifest the desired level of enthusiasm. Since selling is persuading others, especially those on the 'other side of the fence', you have to sound convincing. Collecting the relevant facts and creating the right atmosphere and emotion will help you persuade better.

◆ 6. End as Powerfully as You Begin

The conclusion of your presentation should highlight the specific action you want the client to take. You should close the sale while your presentation is still fresh in the buyer's minds. A week later they would have forgotten all about you as well as the benefits of the product you had touted!

Research shows that if 1000 people are handed a product advertisement in print, this is what would happen:

One day later   : 25 per cent would have forgotten its contents
Two days later   : 50 per cent would have forgotten
Four days later   : 85 per cent would have forgotten
Seven days later : 97 per cent would have forgotten

So strike when the iron is hot!

Barriers to Effective Communication

Having understood the nuances of making an effective sales presentation, it is also essential that you are conscious of the kind of habits or traits that might come in the way of making an impact. These constitute the 'barriers' to an effective presentation and an awareness of these helps to avoid them. A few such barriers are enumerated below.

◆ Vague and General Statements

Many sales persons cut a sorry figure when customers seek detailed information on something stated in the presentation. Prepare thoroughly to avoid such situations. You can also sometimes get carried away and end up promising the moon. Obviously, it would subsequently prove difficult for you to keep your word. You should avoid statements like, '*we give excellent service*' or '*we will help you reduce your costs enormously*'. It is better to promise less and deliver more than the other way round.

◆ Choice of Words and Language

At no point in time should the customer feel threatened. As a seller you might inadvertently use words or phrases which rub the customer the wrong way. For example, phrases such as, '*if I were you*' or '*what I can advise*' are avoidable. The customer is not looking for advice. At the most, you may suggest. The way you present your sales talk goes a long way in helping clinch the deal.

◆ Confusing Facts with Opinions

As a sales professional, you have to understand the basic difference between the features of a product and its benefits as mentioned earlier. Information shared with clients should be based on data and facts. You need to remember that facts are friendly. Only if your opinion is asked for should you venture to give it. But remember never to confuse fact and opinion.

◆ Use of Jargon and Technical Words

Use complex terminology only when necessary. If avoidable, do not focus on product- or service-specific jargon. Try not to confuse the audience. Barriers in communication need to be removed swiftly before any damage is done.

The Equipment and Media Used

Visuals play prominent role in most sales presentations. You could be using a television, a computer, an overhead projector or the simple flipchart and whiteboard. The type of aid used depends on the customer, the facilities available at the venue and the time available for the presentation.

The following are a few points to remember:

- Keep the visuals short and simple. Complicated and cluttered visuals confuse more than clarify. Try and display one idea at a time.
- Whatever the medium, you should be facing the audience most of the time.
- Colour adds to the message. Therefore use colour slides or colour chalks and pens.
- You will have to merge the audio-visuals into your main presentation. Their use should add value to your verbal

message. Practice your presentation to smoothly incorporate the audio-visual element.

- Check the equipment before your presentation. Laptops, projectors and other supporting infrastructure may malfunction. This can be very unnerving if discovered at the last moment.
- Use graphs, pictures and charts wherever possible, substituting them for the written word. Visuals, as we know, are more powerful than simple text.

Handling Questions/Objections

A sales presentation without queries or objections from the customer is unheard of. So be prepared and anticipate the kind of questions you may have to face. The first step is to change your attitude regarding objections. These are actually milestones towards the sale, not a wall with 'no sale' written on it.

Learn how to respond to questions as these are an integral part of sales presentations. There could be objections that you cannot answer. In this case, you should thank the person for having brought up the issue and seek time to explain the matter. If that isn't possible, you need to assertively explain why you cannot help. On the other hand, when a valid objection is raised, you need to first listen carefully to the query and remain as calm as possible while doing so. Try not to interrupt the speaker. The next step is to convert the objection into a question and reply to that question. You could say: '*it seems that the real question is . . .*' or '*so what you are really asking is . . .*' It is important in terms of the sale to seek the customer's agreement to your response. Both parties should operate in tandem to ensure the overall success of such a presentation.

So, before you venture into making a sales presentation, know your customer well, understand his needs and then draft the presentation for his benefit.

13

TELEVISION ARTIST/HOST

Television is one of the most powerful means of mass communication we have today. It is a blend of the audio and the video. A career in the field of television is much sought after, especially after the launch of satellite channels. The glamour associated with the world of television often disguises some of the hard realities of the job. Among a host of skills required, the most important one is probably the ability to communicate effectively.

✦ Communicating through Television Means:

- A cross-section of people will be watching the telecast.
- There exists the possibility of appearing live or on pre-recorded programmes.
- There will be a reduced emphasis on voice quality as compared to radio communication.

- People management and the co-ordination of artists, technicians and actors is critical.
- There will be less reliance on a prepared speech.
- Programmes will be competing with innumerable others being shown on TV simultaneously.
- There exists the possibility of using far more sophisticated visuals.
- Multimedia presentations are possible.

In spite of television being a separate medium, some of the fundamental premises of public speaking hold good here as well. These premises are universal and apply to speakers regardless of the media they use.

Key Abilities

The main skills required to be an effective television host are indicated below:

✦ Language

This is the basic ability required for any job in the media. Your language skills have to be highly developed. You must be fluent and should use the language simply, with short uncomplicated sentences and words that reflect spontaneity.

✦ Publ

This is a valuable skill. It is what separates the TV presenter from the backroom person or the production assistant.

✦ Comfort with Audio-visual Aids

You need to be technology-friendly and able to use the props available to your advantage.

✦ Listening

In interactive programmes, besides speaking, it is equally important to listen to others.

Preparation

The importance of this phase cannot be undermined even in the world of television where takes and retakes are possible. Preparation helps ensure that the programme is wound up with the minimum wastage of resources and with maximum effectiveness. The points to focus on, in this regard, are:

* **Information Optimisation**

You should have all the relevant information on your fingertips including a high level of familiarity with the topic and the guests. This will help make the show interesting. An informed host is confident and able to transform an average show into a top-rated one.

* **Familiarity with Guests on the Show**

A certain degree of familiarity with guests and interviewees will help you prepare questions. You will then be well equipped to extract the best from the guest.

* **Audience Analysis**

A factor that contributes most towards making a television show successful is an understanding of the audience. To stand out among a huge number of similar programmes, the presenter and the production team have to be aware of the nature of the audience and their expectations. A word of caution here: it is highly improbable that a show will appeal to the entire cross-section of people watching television. The production team should target, instead, a particular segment of the audience and tailor the programme according to their tastes.

Presentation

This is the phase when you are in front of the camera conducting the programme. There are a large variety of programmes that you may host and each one of them requires a combination of particular fundamental skills. You could be handling:

Statements to the camera (Point to Camera–PTC).

Interviews of celebrities.

Moderation of major events.

Talk shows.

Movie-based programmes.

Most of these events require dexterity in both public speaking and people management. The presentation skills required in such situations are *verbal/vocal, non-verbal* and *session-specific*. The former includes such areas as choice of words, fluency, clarity, voice modulation and articulation. Non-verbal skills comprise active listening and body language. Session-specific skills would include personal grooming, handling of visuals, and time and people management. Being a television host requires much more than just simple speaking skills.

Verbal and Vocal Skills

◆ Words/Content

The words you use must be well thought out. While some of the material you use will be prepared and edited beforehand, you will have to improvise and ad-lib to a great extent. A word of caution, though. The introduction and conclusion should never be ad-libbed. The introduction is critical and you should plan and choose the most appropriate words for it. The same holds true while winding up a show.

The language should be simple to understand and devoid of jargon unless necessary. Supplement your speech with analogies to illustrate the points you are making. Words should be strung together into short, clear sentences. Words are the basis of informative programmes and have to be focussed on to obtain maximum mileage from them.

◆ Language and Fluency

Fluency in the language being used is essential to ensure that the programme is understood by all. Unwanted accents should be eliminated as you will be catering to a wide cross-section of the audience. Since communicating over the television is a linear process, as against a two way one, highlighting information by reiteration is necessary. This is to avoid misunderstanding.

◆ Delivery

Unlike a presentation in front of a live audience in an auditorium, television modifies the need for voice projection since this can be controlled electronically. The emphasis, therefore, has shifted to the modulation of the voice. Television demands clear enunciation. The pace of delivery has to be appropriate to both remain within the time limit and yet be transmitted clearly.

◆ Clarity and Articulation

This particular point follows from the previous one. However, to emphasize its importance, perhaps a little elaboration is in order. The medium of television demands clear and concise speech which can be transmitted to the viewer to sound as if you are speaking to them directly. Garbled speech ruins the informative content and interest value of the programme. An articulate host succeeds in conveying his message clearly to both the audience and the guest on the show.

Non-Verbal Skills

◆ Active Listening and Empathy

This can be rated the primary requirement for any television host, especially those hosting guest-based shows/interviews. An active host ensures by listening well that all relevant information has been garnered from the guest. Empathy with the interviewee makes him feel at ease often resulting in a much more interesting and insightful programme. This particular trait can also help you gain entry into the otherwise 'out-of-bounds territory' of a guest.

◆ Body Language

The manner in which you conduct yourself, especially in the case of interviews, greatly impacts the value of the presentation being made. A positive and friendly manner, indicated by your body language, is essential. The interest and enthusiasm reflected in your non-verbal communication is imbibed by the audience who then remain focussed on the programme. Negative indicators such as a languid posture, a vacant expression, or restless gestures will make the audience feel that you aren't interested and they will then tune off. Your facial expressions and gestures emphasize important points and make the programme lively. Television favours a relaxed and intimate style and the body language should match this. Some tips to remember in this regard are:

- Seat yourself comfortably, especially while interviewing guests on the show.
- Exercise control over the movement of your hands and head, reducing unnecessary gestures such as rubbing your nose, etc.
- Maintain proper eye contact with the guest.
- Hold your head high. Otherwise poor lighting may make it seem like you have shadows under your eyes.
- Maintain a calm and interested countenance (whatever the nature of the programme being hosted).
- Adopt an alert and open posture.
- Most importantly, imagine you are facing your audience. Don't talk lifelessly to the lens.

Session-Specific Skills

This section includes some important things a television host needs to keep in mind. Neglecting these aspects is bound to create a negative impact.

♦ Personal Grooming

One cannot stress this enough in the context of your assignment as a host. The 'visual' aspect is an important feature you offer and care must be taken to see that the maximum advantage is derived from it. Television is, after all, a viewers medium. A well groomed host conveys the sense of glamour and professionalism required and also sets trends. A badly dressed host conveys a sense of mediocrity. Some of the basic do's and don'ts are:

- Select an attire which reflects the image of the programme.
- Avoid clothes with lumpy textures that may be exaggerated by the camera.
- Wear an outfit that does not distract viewer attention.

- Choose colours that match your skin tone.
- Do not wear fine prints, checks and stripes. These can cause the TV image to disintegrate.
- Avoid wearing trinkets. These can also be distracting.
- Choose simple hairstyles and make sure they do not obscure the face.
- Avoid exaggerated make-up. As the face is magnified and seen at close quarters, and is further enhanced by lights, you need to use appropriate make-up. Smoothen it evenly so that the final texture looks pleasing.
- Check with the production team in advance about all the above if you are a first time presenter.

◆ Time Management

Television programmes are a set of time-bound presentations. Time-management means you should not overshoot or under-shoot the slot allotted for the programme. You have to keep the programme on track and achieve the maximum while making it interesting for the viewer. Possible pitfalls in this area are when the guest is either garrulous or reluctant to talk in which case the objective of the show may not entirely be met. It is up to you as the host, especially in the case of live telecasts, to see that the capsule is appropriate in its content. For pre-recorded programmes too, it is important to manage time well. Although editing the programme later can help, large amounts of editing can make the programme appear unnatural and awkward.

◆ Handling Questions

This is an exceedingly important concern for the television host especially in the case of interviews. These are not questions asked of you but ones you ask the guest. They have to be care-fully thought out in order to make the guest divulge informa-tion. Handling questions well makes the difference between a good show and a bad one.

Unlike the conventional presenter, television hosts have to improvise. Questions asked can range from ones that are open-ended to those that force a choice. The comfort and skill with which you ask the correct question at the correct time adds value to the programme. Sensitivity to your guest is also a factor to be considered and helps you decide what to ask and what not to.

◆ Handling Your Nerves

If you are appearing on television and are not slightly ner-vous, then there is something wrong! Nervousness is natural while facing the camera. Accepting this fact at the outset helps. A few techniques you can use to reduce your anxiety are:

- Breathe deeply and slowly several times before the cameras are switched on.

- Keep some water handy in case you find your mouth drying up.

- Smile as often as possible. This is the best antidote to stress.

- Maintain a positive, open body language. Never cross/fold your arms. Use open, upward palm gestures. Keep your hands, pen and similar props away from your mouth.

Television Interviewee

The other role you could be playing on television could be that of the person being interviewed. The pointers provided for hosts would apply equally to you.

As you are being watched by many people, whatever you say should be well thought out. You could encounter various kinds of questions and you will have to be ready to face them with confidence. Sometimes you may disagree with a value judgement attached to a question. In such a case, you should first smile before you reply and then say something to the effect of 'I can appreciate/understand this point of view but if you look at it another way, then . . .'

Often you may face a question drafted negatively. It is your job to reframe the question and then reply. This can be done by changing the context of the question and saying, for example, 'I wonder if people realise that this is because . . . '

If the interviewer detects an inconsistency or a contradiction in any of your statements, actions or policies, acknowledge it and then go on to your answer. You could say, for instance, 'yes that's true and I would like to emphasize that that is the very reason for our insistence on . . .'

Television is a powerful medium. But a lot depends on how the individual featuring in the programme makes use of it. You either get watched and liked or switched off. So, it is essential to put in adequate effort while preparing for and presenting your programme.

14

RADIO BROADCASTER

In this era of mass communication there is a growing breed of men and women who use Frequency Modulated (FM) Radio Channels to communicate with large audiences. Besides, traditional Amplitude Modulated (AM) radio stations such as All India Radio (AIR) also reach out to vast rural and urban audiences. Contrary to what people think, and in spite of the growth of television, radios are still in vogue and a preferred medium of communication for advertisers who wish to reach their chosen audience.

Communicating with audiences over the radio requires a special set of skills. These skills can be developed and further improved through proper preparation, voice training and a conscious emphasis on one's style of presentation. In this chapter, I intend to cover these aspects in detail.

Preparation

Preparation is critical for a radio broadcaster. The speech or the matter that has to be delivered needs to be rehearsed a number of times to ensure fluency. Use a stopwatch to adhere to prescribed time limits. If you are a DJ (Disc Jockey), you would need to rehearse in conjunction with the radio station's CD (Compact Disc) changer to get the music and the timings right. A good broadcaster usually tries out a number of variations to take care of any eventuality that might crop up in the course of the programme. When a radio show is live, you will need to plan for and take into account all possible slip-ups such as, the CD changer developing a fault during the show or the wrong song being played accidentally. Preparation is best undertaken within the studio premises with a few people as audience, who also serve to provide feedback on various aspects of the communication process.

You must also take care of your voice by avoiding foods that irritate the throat. Gargle with hot water in which a few drops of honey have been added just before going on air. Throat medicines can also be kept handy for the rare occasion when hoarseness suddenly sets in.

The prepared script will need to be followed as far as possible to keep the communication within the prescribed time limit. However, you can add a touch of spontaneity by improvising or 'ad-libbing' during the show. The right balance between a prepared speech and spontaneous interjections, along with appropriate voice changes and modulation form the backbone of your communication.

Key competencies of radio broadcasters are the quality of voice, delivery skill and personal speaking style. You will need to work on all of these to become an adept and effective radio communicator.

Quality of Voice

Apart from the content of a radio presentation, what the

listener of a radio broadcast experiences is the evocative impact of the speaker's voice. You can either retain the attention of the listener by your powerful vocal ability or you can leave him bored and distracted. Being able to modulate and vary your pitch of voice therefore is most essential. Every word should be delivered with clarity and distinctiveness. You cannot either 'gobble up' words or 'dovetail' one word with another. You have to work on your pronunciation. Being fluent in speech, without having to rely on the use of fillers such as 'ah...ah', 'um...' and the like, is necessary. The pace should be just right for people to understand what is being said. Pauses should be kept to a minimum.

A few speech problems that the radio broadcaster will have to guard against are: nasality (which is the tendency to speak through the nose instead of the mouth), shrillness of voice, the

RADIO BROADCASTER

tendency to whisper into the mike instead of throwing the voice out, mumbling (lazy lips), and hoarseness and rasping (tired throat). Asking a few listeners or close friends off the air how your voice comes through would provide valuable feedback. Working on your weaknesses systematically will help improve your speech.

Delivery and Personal Speaking Style

Delivery and your personal speaking style are the secret ingredients that determine your success as a radio broadcaster. Although one cannot undermine the importance of preparation, it is the personal speaking style and quality of the voice of a commentator or disk jockey that makes an impact on the listener. Good broadcasters cultivate a voice for all occasions. Since radio broadcasters use only their voice to create the required effect and stir the desired emotion in the listener, it is important for them to be observant and study how different people speak. Well known broadcasters have the ability to speak in a variety of ways.

Another important aspect related to the efficacy of your broadcast is the ability not to let personal moods reflect in the communication. You may have had a very rough day but it is important to sound fresh and cheerful everytime you are on the microphone.

Effective broadcasters also display a high degree of sensitivity towards their listeners. While reaching out to teenagers, for example, it is important to think with and like them. You have to consciously prevent your beliefs and values from coming in the way of building a rapport with the audience. This is one of the most important aspects of communication through a medium such as the radio.

Problems in Radio Communication

The most critical problems related to radio communication come under two broad categories:

- **Technical problems**
- **Non-technical problems**

1. Technical problems

   Technical problems are the 'gremlins' that have to do with the hardware or software within the studio. You can have problems, for example, with the equipment, with the wrong disk being played, the wrong channel broadcast, or with inferior sound quality. All this has a deleterious impact on the overall communication process.

   It often helps to explain to the listeners the nature of the problem that has cropped up so that they do not fiddle with the settings of their radio sets or switch channels. It is also important to be calm in the face of technical failures. The use of spontaneous humour can help retain a disenchanted audience.

2. Non-technical problems

   Non-technical problems are usually of a personal nature, and can relate to the quality of a broadcaster's voice, to him/her forgetting to bring the script to the studio or bringing the wrong script, reading out the wrong request or mispronouncing names.

   Non-technical problems can be averted by preparing well. This brings us back to the importance of preparation and having a dry run before the show goes on air.

   The radio is facing tough competition from the world of Information Technology and from television, yet it has survived. And will do so in the future. So, if you are made for the radio, make the most of it!

15

TRAINERS AND FACILITATORS

People involved in training and development need to communicate extensively. Your role as a change agent and facilitator of learning requires you to be fluent and in full charge of your verbal repertoire. Your role is to translate complex concepts into simple, easily understandable ideas. All would agree that the learning acquired from a lecture, seminar or training workshop bears a direct relationship with the individual delivering the inputs or facilitating the learning. The other day, I inquired of a friend how a particular presentation was. He exclaimed that it was *superb*! He had just heard a talk from an expert on 'competitiveness'. When I probed further to find out what made the lecture 'superb', I heard words and phrases like, 'simple', jargon-free, 'lots of analogies', 'informal' and 'relaxed ambience' that explained what made the talk special. Isn't this something that would appeal to all listeners?

TRAINERS/FACILITATORS

If your profession requires you to lecture, facilitate learning or conduct workshops to impart skills or knowledge, then it would be worthwhile to go through the next few pages carefully, since I believe that mastering the art of communication is essential for all such professionals to be effective.

The basics of good speaking have been dealt with completely in Parts One and Two of the book. The essential features of effective speaking remain the same for trainers and facilitators. Our attention must now focus on understanding the barriers that we inadvertently create in our efforts to reach out to the audience in the course of our interactions.

BARRIERS TO COMMUNICATION

No trainer deliberately creates barriers. However, as every skilful trainer knows, a variety of internal and external factors can affect the quality of the learner's experience. Communicating effectively requires a thorough understanding of these barriers because awareness is the first step towards surmounting them.

Barrier 1: The Training Ambience

There could be conditions in the physical surroundings which create barriers. You cannot expect all training to take place in air-conditioned rooms with the best of seating and other modern infrastructural facilities. However, you can definitely pay attention to details at the venue to improve the quality of the overall presentation.

Preparing for a lecture implies taking care of the various aspects of the room in which the presentation is taking place. This could include particulars such as the floor covering, the blinds on the windows, a proper black- or whiteboard with adequate chalk and colour pens, a comfortable seating arrangement, as well as the sound and the light arrangements in the room. Imagine conducting a two-day workshop where your participants are sitting on uncomfortable tin chairs with no tables in front of them, and where the trainer expects them to fill questionnaires and take notes! You, as the lecturer, could be at your best but there is already a stumbling block to impede your movement forward. Planning for all this may seem prosaic but it is the small things, that when put together, make up the complete story. I remember conducting a class, one hot Indian summer day, in an air-conditioned venue, but alas! there was no drinking water available! My throat was dry and even the audience was looking around for the tumblers, a familiar sight at most well organized training venues.

It is your responsibility as a speaker to insist on proper arrangements and to plan for them in advance, so that the ambience is pleasant and the setting comfortable for all.

Barrier 2: The Group Size

Speaking to ten people or to ten thousand is not the same. A small group would need a relatively small place to accommodate them and then you may not need a microphone to reach out to them. As a trainer, you could plan for some interactive games or simulations such as role-play to enhance the effectiveness of your task. But the moment you are expected to speak to an auditorium full of people, you will accordingly have to decide on the best way to reach out to them. This would include paying due attention to eye contact, tone of voice, and your overall movement and gestures. If these aspects are ignored, they can prove a formidable barrier.

Barrier 3: Wrong Assumptions

In most relationships, assumptions possess the potential to play havoc. A trainer-trainee bond can also suffer if either one banks on assumptions which have no basis in reality. As a trainer, you may not know much about the group you are addressing. While this could mean having insufficient information on the expectations of the audience or their level of understanding, it would be unadvisable to simply make assumptions.

Being in the dark about these factors can create a barrier between you and the people on the other side. If you do have time, you must conduct a little research and determine as much as you can about the group. This includes the qualifications of its members, their likely concerns, their backgrounds and all else that would help you decide what to include in your presentation.

Whenever I have the opportunity to interact with the organizers of a speech or a presentation that I am making, I find myself asking questions about the audience and thereby clarifying almost everything I want to know about them. This enhances my 'levels of comfort'. Besides, knowing what the audience is looking for from their interaction with me helps me prepare and I then don't have to make wild guesses or depend on assumptions. This approach, of making relevant inquiries about the audience and their expectations, also communicates your commitment to the assignment.

Barrier 4: Psychological Blocks

In a trainer's role, speakers can sometimes alienate their listeners. As a trainer, you may definitely be an expert in your area and know much more about it than your audience. This fact if 'rubbed in' with insensitivity, however, can make the audience withdraw into its 'shell'. And, if you happen to belong to that tribe of speakers who gives considerably more weightage to their speaking skills and knowledge than to the listener's feeling and concerns, you are sure to lose out in terms of forging a rapport with the audience. It should be your endeavour to build bridges between yourself and the audience by communicating with empathy and sensitivity. You need to go out of your way to develop an open, informal climate within which the audience, or the learners can forge a bond with you. This enables you to offer them guidance and support without them really feeling that you are doing so. That is the essence of creating an excellent learning ambience: the learner's sense of self-worth is not diminished and the facilitator is able to forge a close bond with him/her.

The quality of your communication, both verbal and non-verbal, would impact how learners perceive you. The physical management of space, whether you sit or stand, conveys a great deal about you. Over and above this, your facial expressions and the kind of eye contact you maintain with the audience also communicates a number of subtle things about you. What also counts immensely, of course, is the verbal content of your presentation. Together, these factors determine the quality of the relationship you build with your trainees.

Barrier 5: Inappropriate Medium

If the message has to be effective, then the medium for conveying the message must be appropriately selected and aligned with the objectives of the presentation. In fact it has rightly been said that the *medium is the message*.

A company executive was asked to speak to a large but

heterogeneous gathering of ladies who had assembled because they wished to know more about the initiatives taken by the corporation in his area. The executive showed one transparency after another, giving details in a tabular form in addition to presenting a mass of cold and impersonal statistics. I was present too, and I could read from the expressions on faces and uneasiness prevailing in the group that he was not able to reach out to or forge a comfortable relationship with the audience. The speaker had good command over his language but unfortunately what he chose to communicate to the group did not go down well. After his presentation was over, it was left to the CEO of the corporation to translate these facts and figures for the audience.

Barrier 6: Improper Style of Delivery

The average attention span of a listener is about twenty minutes. After this period, the listener's mind starts wandering. Depending on the personal delivery style of a presenter however, this span can either be reduced or increased. As a trainer you need to develop your speaking abilities by being self-aware and practising consistently. You could record your voice on a tape recorder or get yourself videotaped to demonstrate your personal strengths and weaknesses as a speaker. Once you know which of your skills need improvement and change, you can work on it/them systematically.

I, personally, have to be extra careful about my pace so that it does not overtake the group's pace of comprehension. With consistent effort I have now been able to reduce my rate of speech so that my listeners are able to comprehend completely what I say. In fact, I have learned to force myself to take a few well-planned pauses, which is the time my audience use to think and absorb what I have been saying. You will also have to pay attention to the volume of your voice (whether it is loud or low) and its tone (friendly and warm as against curt and formal). All these attributes improve with practice. Interestingly, I am convinced that the better you get as a person, the better trainer or teacher you become. Your desire to learn and develop yourself, therefore, goes hand in hand with your desire to become effective at training others.

Barrier 7: Unstructured Material

If you had experience teaching a child the English alphabet, you would have realized that it is better to start with *ABC* and proceed to *XYZ*. This logical structure simplifies the material being taught. And this is exactly what trainers need to keep in mind while sequencing their content. The bottom line is that the listener should be able to comprehend and assimilate what is coming her way. Only then is the trainer's role effective. This structuring obviously cannot be done while delivering the talk. It needs prior planning and preparation to determine what the introduction, the body and the concluding part of your presentation will be. As mentioned earlier, when you fail to prepare, you are preparing to fail!

Being in the field of training means communicating most of the time. When you are focussed on your topic, sincere to your audience and enjoy interacting with people, there is no stopping you from making a positive, wholesome impact. Working on your ability to express yourself is a continuous process. With each successive cycle of improvement, you will notice a qualitative change in the way the audience responds to you. So, keep learning while helping others learn.

16

ADVERTISING EXECUTIVE

An advertising executive could be making both internal and external presentations. Internal presentations basically serve the purpose of idea-sharing and brainstorming and are highly informal. External presentations can be of three types: *strategic*, *ideational* or *creative*.

A strategic presentation is one in which certain communication strategies are suggested to the client. An ideational presentation is in the form of an intermediate presentation where new ideas are shared with the client and feasible alternatives are jointly sorted out. The creative presentation is the final presentation to a client and dwells on such details as the creative use of various media to promote a product, service or an idea.

For external presentations, the audience can range from the Brand Management team to the Vice President (Marketing) or CEO of the client company. For internal presentations, the audience constitutes the internal strategy team, the Accounts Executives, the creative team, the production group and other members who might be involved with delivering advertising services.

The factor that needs to be kept in mind while making presentations to external clients is the objective of the presentation. This should be absolutely clear to you as the presenter. External presentations are usually formal and aimed specifically at addressing client needs. On the other hand, internal presentations are characterized by more interactions, a sense of informality and an absence of hard selling.

The main difference between advertising presentations and other sales presentations is that advertisers are not selling tangibles but ideas. You must recognize that an advertising strategy for a product or service has to fit in with the client's marketing approach. This implies that to some extent the ideas being sold have to be germane to the client's needs.

You have to be articulate and have the ability to convert ideas into words and visuals with impact. You need to empathize with the client and understand the relevance of the proposed campaign. You should be able to provide advice on the most optimal media solutions.

The structuring of advertising presentations is usually product-based, focussing on how the adoption and use of a certain advertising strategy is likely to woo the consumer. The presentation often focusses on the problems or issues under consideration and then states likely solutions. The compare-and-contrast method can also be used, where the product being advertised is assessed against something already available. Care has to be taken that no other brand name is wilfully attacked. That could result in legal problems. If a totally new product is being launched, then the content and the structuring of the presentation have to be specifically developed. The right words have to be used: words that can persuade and sell the idea to the client. As for all good presentations, the overall sequence should be systematic and easy to follow.

Preparation

Presentations by advertising personnel, like all other presentations are amenable to benefit from preparation. Clients look at advertisers as their 'extended arm' and their expectations are largely satisfied when advertisers make well-prepared presentations. They know that the campaign is in safe hands and will be delivered well if the advertisers can create the desired effect.

Client-servicing executives often make presentations alone, where the onus of making a success of it rests entirely on him/her. However, most presentations involve other team members, especially in the run up to the final act. They may not have to accompany the presenter for all the 'dry runs' but interaction with the client's representatives does no harm. The creative team members can speak about their ideas and present them directly to the client if need be.

A few important points to be borne in mind during preparation relate to the audience, the material, the speaker's style, and audio-visual aids. These points are clarified below.

◆ Audience

Finding out the core strengths of the enterprise whose executives are being addressed, is necessary. This helps to zoom in, quickly and efficiently, on the needs of the client. It is also important to identify the decision-makers in the client organization and get prior information about them, if possible. You need to observe their non-verbal signals during the dry run, to gauge how the information being presented is being received. Maintaining eye contact with all in the audience, and not just the top shot, is essential. Usually, most advertising agencies keep personal dossiers about their clients which provide valuable, relevant information that can be used while preparing a presentation. Making a presentation that addresses the client's concerns adequately helps to build trust and strengthen an advertiser's relationship with the client.

♦ Material

The material used for presentation should be well structured and appropriately planned. Presentations suggestive of illogical, unsystematic thought processes cannot be allowed in professional situations. Having the necessary information/pamphlets/brochures available and at hand is essential. The quality of the write-ups and visuals being used should be excellent. There is no room for any lapses or snafus. Preparing well involves research, analyzing the data collected and spending sufficient time brainstorming and ideating with colleagues. The presentation should be rehearsed along with all the audio-visual material intended for use. Spare copies of brochures/details should be available for the client. They may need to share this information, with their superiors on your behalf. Empower the client through information. In the long run, it helps.

♦ Personal Style

This is extremely important. You must work on yourself and develop a natural style. Formality is essential. While making presentations, besides focussing on your speech, it is essential to spend time listening to what the client has to say. Being alert for information will be beneficial.

One attribute that others appreciate is the capacity to stick to deadlines. This is especially true while presenting one's views to clients. It is critical to keep your word. Getting back on time with the relevant information that the client expects always helps create a positive image of you and your enterprise.

Even deciding what to wear has an impact. A simple secret, let in on by a friend in this field, is to 'look like them'. Knowing which client you are serving helps. An orthodox client would dress up a little more conservatively than his dynamic, younger generation counterpart. As a presenter, you need to assess this and adapt your style accordingly. More important than this, however, is your comfort level. You shouldn't end up dressing like them and in the process, feeling uneasy and restless! That would definitely hamper your objective of making an effective presentation!

Another aspect that you should take care of is the use of jargon. The terminology (or patois) that you are so familiar with, and which you use amongst your colleagues, may not be known to your client. You have to take extra care to avoid the use of jargon.

✦ Audio-visual Aids

Technical audio-visual support, such as laptop computers, video players, multimedia, and projection systems, are being increasingly used in the 'ad' world. Familiarity with the equipment that you intend using during a presentation is imperative. These gadgets do have a high probability of failing, so you have to check and rehearse the presentation along with these aids, to be doubly sure. Sometimes the software used in particular equipments may not be compatible with the clients' system. To be on the safe side, you should carry your own equipment or try the one that is available beforehand.

Handling Questions

While tackling argumentative or hostile questions, the secret is: 'Don't argue'. Never say or even imply that the questioner is wrong. Begin by suggesting that the questioner's point of view and ideas are perfectly legitimate but under the circumstances discussed, your firm would like to present another point of view. Then put forward your argument. You have to learn to defend your stand with facts and data. If the questioner supplies contradictory data, then it may be difficult to verify the authenticity of such data readily. In this case, it helps to state the sources of your data and tell the questioner that you will check his information and get back to him later. The presenter should understand the questioner's need to boost his ego and, therefore, handle the situation courteously and politely, but firmly if necessary.

Gathering Feedback

No formal feedback is generally solicited after advertising presentations. Feedback is gathered, instead, from the subtle reactions of the clients during the presentation and from the informal chats that follow.

The world of advertising is expanding, more so after the launch of satellite television and the growth of the world wide web. Making the most of the media available is the advertisers job. And making effective presentations is a vital function of advertising executives. Acquiring the skills of speaking and developing them continuously is, therefore, essential to succeed in this field.

Appendices

Appendix A

CROSS-CULTURAL SENSITIVITY: THE ESSENCE OF GLOBAL EFFECTIVENESS

Today, businesses have ceased to cater to just the local market. The current boom in the Information Technology sphere coupled with the government's liberalization policies, have come to mean growing interactions on a global scale.

Of course, it is imperative that you possess the technical know-how and knowledge but more importantly, you must be confident and work on and improve your communication skills.

While talking to a senior executive working in an IT firm, I learnt that there was another facet related to communication that needed honing. His firm was offering software solutions to clients in a number of foreign countries besides those who were being served nationally. This young breed of computer professionals, working with overseas clients, often had difficulties interacting with them because they were not adept at making presentations suited to a different cultural milieu. Presentation skills include the ability to relate, respect and deal with others with poise and care.

While the earlier chapters in this book focus on all the necessary tools and techniques needed for good presentations, there are certain special skills you would need to develop to become a capable presenter across global boundaries. Today's global managers, for instance, rely heavily on laptop computers and presentation software to make their presentations. You would therefore need to be comfortable handling PCs or laptop computers, apart from the equipment used to project the monitor display onto a screen. The specific details on the effective use of audio-visual equipment have been covered in Chapter 9.

Global professionals involved in selling software or other products, services or solutions to various transnational organizations will have to develop the personality traits of an effective salesperson. Selling is a skill, and one needs to be sensitive to the customer's expectations and requirements to be effective. I have included a separate segment on presentations for **Sales** professionals. Reading through that section will help you enhance your selling skills and focus on the nuances of making a successful sales presentation.

In this segment, however, I will focus on a very relevant and important aspect of business dealings today: namely, cross cultural sensitivity in the interaction with overseas customers, collaborators or business associates.

It has been proved beyound doubt that being successful today requires not only a mastery of one's job but also of the common courtesies that go with interacting with others. What is required is sensitivity, empathy and the ability to demonstrate concern and consideration for others. You might be an expert in your field but if you cannot interact easily with the people around you, you are unlikely to achieve rapid advancement in your profession. Some managers can, in the short-term, get away with being efficient without having any etiquette; by the same token there are also others who display etiquette but no efficiency or effectiveness in their profession. The best approach, and the one that works wonders, is a blend of the two. Efficiency 'performs', while etiquette enhances the quality of the performance.

Lack of etiquette and grace shows up in the presentation. The professional in question may be good looking, well dressed and presentable, but one act of improper behaviour can ruin the entire impact he/she has created by his/her external charm.

It is a difficult task to be able to handle new situations with aplomb and confidence. There will always be occasions when one is not certain what response would be ideal. In such an event, it helps to learn to operate with calm and use one's common sense to overcome the unforeseen eventuality.

When travelling to different parts of the world, your experience will be enhanced if you know how to socialize and converse with people. Getting to know people is important. It demonstrates that even though people from different lands look different, or speak a different tongue, they too are human, and cherish the same values. This realization builds confidence and enables professionals to feel at ease in different settings.

You can communicate your warmth and friendliness to people in different cultures, and cultivate lasting friendships, through the following actions:

- Asking questions that show you are interested in starting a dialogue.

- Trying to start a conversation with a person whose body language communicates openness and friendliness.

- Avoiding personal remarks or asking personal questions.

- Listening actively. A verbal nod, eye contact and the right questions confirm and show that you are attentive to what the other person is saying.

- Shifting from the use of egocentric phrases such as '*I did*' '*I know*', '*I would say*', to asking the other person open-ended questions through which he can furnish information about himself.

- Saying something in a manner that reflects sensitivity towards the other person. The same thing can be said in different ways. The choice of words is important. Instead of saying '*you are wrong*', you can choose to say, '*I don't agree with this*', and gain a friend in the process!

- Offering compliments. Take care to communicate only what you genuinely feel, otherwise your words could sound like flattery, which everyone can see through, and nobody likes.

Gaining friends is a good beginning. But with the world increasingly turning into a 'global village', you need to be extremely sensitive about cross–cultural interaction. There are certain specific cues or norms that contribute to cross-cultural etiquette. The following is a list of a few pointers to be kept in mind during cross-cultural interaction.

- Use the right hand or both hands to pass things over or receive them.
- Be aware of the norms of behaviour in a specific country. You will have to find out what is considered acceptable and what is not.
- Try not to misinterpret or overreact to the use of certain kinds of words, sounds or gestures in another language. Gloss over something that sounds unpleasant or seems out of place. Ignoring such things is better then creating a scene.
- Every country or area has its own beliefs and values. It is important that, in the role of a guest (outsider), you respect these differences. You need not *adopt* the attitudes held by people of different cultures, but you positively need to *accept* these when you are with them. The status of women, for instance, differs from society to society. However, some values are universal. Mothers all around the globe are worthy of respect. By the same token, you have to protect a child in danger irrespective of which land you are in.
- Use your words carefully. Also, keep a check on your habits, food and otherwise. The saying, 'While in Rome do as the Romans do', is very apt.
- Your expectations of hospitality may not be met completely in another country. This doesn't necessarily imply any disrespect. Levels of hospitality vary from place to place.

There are a few other things you should keep in mind:

- Don't indulge in gossip.
- Don't use abusive language or tell offensive jokes.
- Don't try to dominate discussions.
- Don't be overly courteous.
- Don't speak without proper articulation, clarity or distinctiveness.

- Don't forget to thank your host/hostess before leaving a party or get-together.

Developing your personality is a continuous process. All it needs is a consistent and committed choice to change. Being aware and sensitive to the process of improvement, and to events around, is a helpful way to get a head start.

AVOIDING THE PITFALLS OF IMPROPER PROTOCOL

Protocol, as defined by the Random House Dictionary of the English Language, is the set of customs and regulations dealing with diplomatic formality, precedence and etiquette. Professionals who travel the globe have to be aware of the customs and regulations that apply in different parts of the world. Below are some tips that specify the norms for the particular region.

Protocol Tips for Europe

- The business attire for men is a suit or blazer and tie; for women a suit, dress, or elegant blouse and skirt.

- One has to endeavour to be on time for meetings, even though in southern Europe you may occasionally be kept waiting.

- Shake hands when meeting people and again when leaving.

- Use surnames until explicitly told to do otherwise. In most European countries, use the person's title, such as 'Frau Doktor' in Germany or 'Commendatore' in Italy.

- While kissing on the cheeks and hugging are common in many European countries, visitors should not initiate these gestures.

- Business gifts are not an essential part of European business culture.

- It is considered appropriate to discuss business over lunch. At dinner, wait for your counterpart to bring up the subject. 'Power breakfasts' are still rare in most of Europe.

Protocol Tips for Asia

- Men should wear a dark suit and tie to show respect in Japan, South Korea and China, while a white shirt and tie are acceptable for meetings in South-East Asia. Women should wear a dress or business suit, long-sleeved silk blouse, and below-the-knee skirt in South-East Asia. South Asia is generally warm and the dresses one wears must be suited to the conditions and be sufficiently comfortable.

- Wear loafers and a good pair of socks—you will need to take off your shoes in private homes and often on factory visits.

- Meeting and greeting rituals vary countrywise. Non-Asian visitors often look awkward trying to bow in East Asia. Instead, nod your head slightly while shaking hands or clasping your hands in a 'namaste' or 'wai' gesture.

- Expect little or no physical contact beyond a handshake.

- Use family names and titles. In East Asia, the family name precedes the personal name. South-East Asians may call you by your first name preceded by 'Mr', 'Mrs', 'Dr', so you might be addressed as 'Mr Bob' or 'Mrs Mary.'

- Business gifts are important, especially in Japan, China and Korea. The choice of gift and the proper way of presenting it, however, varies.

- Business guests can expect to be lavishly entertained. It is customary to reciprocate with a dinner invitation. Ask for local advice on where to host your function.

Protocol Tips for Latin America

- The business attire for men is a suit or blazer and tie; for women a fashionable suit, dress, or blouse and skirt.

- Try to be on time for meetings even though you might be kept waiting.

- Shake hands firmly when meeting and again when leaving.

- Use family names until invited to switch to first names. Use a person's academic or professional title, such as 'Doctor Morales', 'Director Reyes', or 'Professor Santana.' Remember that a person's 'middle' name is part of his or her family name.

- Business gifts are important, but the choice of the gift and how to present it varies. Again, seek local advice if possible.

- Visitors should stay at prestigious hotels, not downmarket ones, and entertain customers at highly regarded restaurants.

Today's professionals have to be able to travel the globe with ease. Crossing the 'seven seas' may have been rare in the past but not so today. A professional today cannot escape exposure to foreign cultures. There is nothing to fear, and if one is concerned about the social norms of a place, let me assure you that etiquette and social graces *are* learnable provided one is willing to try. It would be a mistake to give up an opportunity to travel overseas because you are anxious about how you should deal with your business partners. Well thought out initiatives in a particular direction in your life will only make you more comfortable in that area. The same holds true of cross-cultural interaction.

Appendix B

COMMUNICATING BAD NEWS

Speakers have to contend with a variety of situations. Speaking to large audiences implies that there will be amplified feedback based on what is communicated to them. If something pleasant is conveyed, there is bound to be a wholesome, positive response. If something harsh is spoken of, the speaker needs to be prepared for an outburst of spontaneous feelings that can derail the speech.

If the tidings were always good, managers would face no difficulty in communicating them. Good news, whatever form it is put across in, sounds good. The news that someone is going to get a raise or a promotion will always be welcomed pleasantly, notwithstanding how it was put across.

Unfortunately, there aren't always pleasant tidings to be shared. Trying to balance the requirements of investors, customers, employees, and the general public, can result in having to communicate uncomfortable and painful news.

With competition hotting up in most sectors, the need of the hour is downsizing and the cutting of costs. This often finds the manager communicating bad news to his subordinates.

The ancient Greeks had a simple method of dealing with bad news: they just killed the messenger who brought it! To avoid a similar fate, managers need to be sensitive to the impact of unwelcome news. It wouldn't be proper to expect people to respond with delight to the news that their services have been terminated. It is equally tough on the manager to convey this harsh information to someone with whom he may have shared strong bonds at the workplace. All the same, however unpleasant the message is, you can play a vital role in handling the communication.

A few important considerations that you need to keep in mind are outlined below:

- Know very specifically and clearly what you are going to communicate. The information should be complete and spell out clearly the various aspects of the message. Do not try to confuse the listener, so that he/she doesn't understand the real implications of the message. Focus on the facts instead of giving your opinion.

- Put yourself in the receiver's situation and empathize with him/her. Understand what your message can mean to him/her. Try and gather all the relevant information in connection with what you are about to say. You can then deliver the 'entire picture', including the pros and the cons, and thereby soften the impact.

- On receiving negative, upsetting messages, people are bound to respond with negative emotions like anger, fear, frustration, blame or hurtful sullenness. Accepting these reactions as natural, without labelling them irrational, helps. You will have to show abundant respect for the feelings and experience of the person concerned.

- When you are communicating with you subordinate, you

are doing so on behalf of your department and organization. It is unprofessional to blame your superiors for taking harsh decisions. An effective manager should avoid creating such an atmosphere.

- Try and be as calm and considerate as possible. If you handle the conversation with poise and possess a relaxed attitude, chances are that the message will be received with ease. If you are ruffled and ready to defend yourself even before you start, you are sending out signals which are not beneficial in such situations.

- You don't merely have to express your point of view. Keep the channel open for communication. It makes the listener feel heard and respected. If there is any kind of professional support that you can organize for the person, do so.

Leaving him/her in the lurch is uncalled for. You should speak to the personnel department on behalf of the concerned person to garner valuable information that he/she can use.

- Lastly don't try to sugar the pill. If the news is unpleasant, it is best delivered in an honest, straightforward manner. This approach is preferable to a meek attempt to distort the truth or project a diluted version of the facts. People like to hear things the way they are, rather than be handed out sops.

So, even if the news is unpleasant, you can help deliver it in a way which is acceptable to your listener/s.

SELECT BIBLIOGRAPHY

Bennet, Roger. *Personal Effectiveness*. London: Kogan Page, 1994.

Beuchner, Frederick. "Speaking with Style" by Carl Wayne Hensley. *American Speaker*. Washington D.C.: Georgetown, Sept/Oct. 1996. 5.

Braude, Jacob M. *Speakers' Encyclopaedia of Humour*. Mumbai: Jaico, 1998.

Goldmann, Heinz. *Communicate to Win: 12 Key Points for Success*. London: Pitman, 1995.

Leeds, Dorothy. *Power Speak: The Complete Guide to Public Speaking and Presentation*. New York: Piatkus, 1990.

Mandel, Steve. *Effective Presentation Skills: A Practical Guide for Better Speaking*. California: Crisp, 1993.

Newman, Edwin. *Strictly Speaking*. London: W.H. Allen, 1975.

————. "Speaking with Style" by Carl Wayne Hensley. *American Speaker*. Washington D.C.: Georgetown, Sept/Oct. 1996. 5.

Pemberton, Maria. *Effective Speaking*. London: Industrial Society, 1991.

Stevens, Michael. *Improving your Presentation Skills*. London: Kogan Page, 1990.

Tierney, Elizabeth P. *How to Make Effective Presentations*. California: Sage, 1995.

Whalen, D. Joel. *I See What You Mean: Persuasive Business Presentations*. California: Sage, 1996.

INDEX

ABOUT THE AUTHOR

Savita Bhan Wakhlu is presently Director and Head, Jagriti Communications, Jamshedpur. Earlier, she worked as the Resident Consultant in Jamshedpur for the Pragati Consulting Group, Pune. For the last twelve years, she has trained over twenty thousand corporate executives, engineers, bureaucrats, professionals, and students in the art of public speaking and interpersonal communication. She is a visiting faculty member at XLRI, Jamshedpur and the Indian Institute of Coal Management (IICM), Ranchi. Her training interventions have benefited organizations such as Tata Steel, Larsen and Toubro, Voltas, IDBI, Philips, TCS, and Jindal Steel. An engineer by training, Savita Wakhlu has also taught at the Regional Engineering College, Srinagar. She is a committed Rotarian, besides being an active theatre person, a radio broadcaster, and a regular columnist for the Jamshedpur edition of the *Telegraph*.